LAW OF EXTRACURRICULAR ACTIVITIES IN SECONDARY SCHOOLS

BY

J. DAVID MOHLER

Associate Professor of Education
The University of West Florida
Pensacola, Florida

AND

EDWARD C. BOLMEIER

Professor of Education
Duke University
Durham, North Carolina

AMERICAN SCHOOL LAW SERIES

Cincinnati

THE W. H. ANDERSON COMPANY

FOREWORD

On the basis of cases referred to in this publication it is evident that extracurricular activities, and particularly competitive athletics, are in a state of confusion and dubiety. A number of the activities which are permitted and conducted in the public schools fall in the "twilight zone" as far as their legal place in the public school program is concerned.

It is not for the courts to decide what shall constitute a school program and how it shall be managed. That is the responsibility of the legislature and the legally constituted public school officials to whom authority is delegated. The judiciary is reluctant to interfere with their prerogatives. The primary function of the court in cases involving extracurricular activities is whether their inclusion, administration, and support are in harmony with state constitutional provisions. Within constitutional and statutory limits, the school boards have the authority and responsibility to decide what shall be included in extracurricular, as well as curricular, programs.

It is the intention of the authors that the court cases reported in this book, and the resulting legal principles derived therefrom, as stated briefly in Chapter 7, will be helpful to those who make school laws, rules, and regulations regarding the complete school program. It is not so important whether the activities of the school are referred to as "extras" or not. The main concern should be that they are legal and that they fulfill the purposes for which the public schools are established and supported.

TABLE OF CONTENTS

Chapter 1: INTRODUCTION

Section

Chapter 2: AUTHORITY OF SCHOOL DISTRICTS TO PROVIDE EXTRACURRICULAR FACILITIES

Chapter 3: LEGALITY OF RULES AND REGULATIONS CONCERNING THE PARTICIPATION OF PUBLIC SCHOOL PUPILS IN EXTRACURRICULAR ACTIVITIES

Chapter 4: LEGAL AUTHORITY OF ATHLETIC ASSOCIATIONS TO CONTROL EXTRACURRICULAR ACTIVITIES

Chapter 5: LEGAL CONSIDERATIONS INVOLVING TEACHERS ASSIGNED TO EXTRACURRICULAR ACTIVITIES

Chapter 6: TORT LIABILITY AS RELATED TO EXTRACURRICULAR ACTIVITIES

Chapter 7: CONCLUDING SUMMARY

Chapter 1

INTRODUCTION

§ 1.1   Variation in terminology and purpose

The vagueness of the real meaning of "extracurricular" activities has been the cause of considerable confusion and dispute. The term "extracurricular" is largely the cause for the vagueness. The prefix "extra" denotes a school program with extraneous features beyond the scope for which a public school is properly and legally responsible.

Because of the criticism of the term, "extracurricular," numerous educators and writers employ modified terms which may be conceived as more justifiable for activities to be carried on in the public school program. Some of the terms which are found in the literature are "allied activities," "extraclass activities," "cocurricular activities," and "student activities." It is doubtful that these modified terms have altered purposes of the activities.

Regardless of the terminology for school activities, the real and legal purpose of the public school is to provide an educational program for the maximum proper development for all youth. Whether or not this objective may be achieved by a curriculum without "extras" will depend upon the breadth of the curriculum concept. On the one extreme, there are those who conceive the curriculum to be only an array of subjects or courses for which credit is allowed in terms of "Carnegie units." On the other extreme, some view the curriculum as all experiences offered youth under the aegis of the school. With this latter interpretation of the curriculum, the term "extracurricular" would be superfluous. Also, in all probability, much of the misunderstanding and litigation regarding the proper and legal responsibility of the public school would diminish.

1

The inclusion in the school programs of student activities with objectives other than those which are educational may be questioned with respect to their propriety and legality. Conversely, the omission of those activities which contribute to the maximum development of youth raises the question as to whether or not the public schools provide the experiences expected by those who patronize and support them.

In the foreword of a 1965 publication dealing with student activities in the North Carolina public schools, the Superintendent of Public Instruction, Charles F. Carroll, succinctly states the purpose of student activities in the total curriculum: ". . .Unless student activities contribute positively toward the well-balanced growth and development of youth, they miss their avowed purposes and cannot be justified. On the other hand, unless the curriculum affords opportunities for student activities, many students will be deprived of those experiences that would enrich their lives."[1]

As far as the purpose of this publication is concerned it seems unnecessary to depart from the original terminology (extracurricular activities). Until school administrators and boards of education consider interscholastic athletic teams, school bands, student clubs, and other out-of-class organizations as educationally significant enough to support them entirely with public funds, they should be regarded as extracurricular. No matter how great their contribution to the total educational experiences of the students, they are outside of the curriculum administratively. Therefore, the term "extracurricular" is used in this book because it is generally understood and most precisely defines the out-of-class activities herein discussed: those activities not fiscally supported by public funds.

§ 1.2   Legal authority over extracurricular activities

Usually the state constitution charges the state legislature with the authority and responsibility to establish and control the public school system. Therefore it may be concluded

1 Raymond K. Rhodes and Vester M Mulholland, Student Activities. State of North Carolina, Department of Public Instruction, Raleigh, Publication No. 375, February 1965. Foreword.

that, within constitutional limits, state legislatures have plenary authority with respect to matters of policy for the public school curriculum—even in the broadest sense of the curriculum where the various student activities are included.

In rare instances, state constitutions provide for specific inclusions in the curriculum. In no state constitution, however, is reference made to what may be regarded as an extracurricular activity.

Virtually every state has enacted legislation requiring certain subject matters to be included in the public school curriculum. Even though state statutes are not likely to specifically require extracurricular activities to be included in the school program, some do stipulate the manner of their control. The law of North Carolina is illustrative:

> County and city boards of education shall make all rules and regulations necessary for the conducting of extracurricular activities in the schools under their supervision, including a program of athletics, where desired, without assuming liability therefor; provided, that all interscholastic athletic activities shall be conducted in accordance with rules and regulations prescribed by the State Board of Education.[2]

Most of the statutes like that of North Carolina, quoted above, pertaining to the school program, are rather general—as they should be—with delegated authority to state boards of education, local boards of education, or professional school personnel to determine the specifics.

Where local boards of education are permitted or mandated to make rules and regulations governing extracurricular activities, it is important that they act in accordance with the constitutional and statutory provisions of the state and the prescriptions of the state board of education, where it is authorized by statute to prescribe rules.

> In view of the fact that the legal responsibility for the operation of the public schools rests with county and city boards of education, it becomes increasingly clear that

---

[2] Id., p. 3.

such boards should have clearcut policies, rules, and regulations relative to organization, administration,and supervision of all school activities, including student activities. . . .As local policies, rules, and regulations are formulated, care should be taken to see that they conform with regulations and standards prescribed by the State Board of Education.[3]

If school authorities would heed the above suggestions, much of the potential misunderstanding and litigation pertaining to extracurricular activities could be avoided.

§ 1.3 Scope of extracurricular consideration

This publication is primarily concerned with case law pertaining to the various aspects of extracurricular activities in the secondary school. Cases which pertain exclusively to curricular considerations such as litigation involving the physical education courses are not discussed, except to illustrate points of law which apply equally to the extracurricular as well as to the curricular program.

Some courts regard what is customarily accepted by school authorities as extracurricular to be part of the regular school curriculum. Such cases are discussed here, for the subject of litigation is within the scope of the meaning of extracurricular activities herein defined: out—of—class activities which do not receive total financial support from the board of education. Although some schools might provide total financial support for activities such as band, which is frequently classified as extracurricular by many schools, no distinction is made, for the actual status of the various activities is not always indicated in the court reports.

Dissenting opinions, when they exist, are presented only if they are germane to the extracurricular question involved in the case, or if some significant legal principle is discussed.

For the purpose of illustration, cases other than those dealing exclusively with extracurricular questions are

---

[3] Id., p. 3.

cited to document certain legal principles. However, an exhaustive, comprehensive documentation by cases to illustrate various legal points is not attempted.

Since this book is mainly concerned with legal principles growing out of court decisions, statutes are not cited except when it is necessary to do so in order to understand a particular case, or for the purpose of providing introductory information for the various topics discussed.

The litigation discussed is restricted to cases which came before the federal and state appellate courts, except for a few lower court cases which illustrate significant legal points in relation to extracurricular activities.

The coverage of this book may be determined from the chapter headings. It may be noted that only those cases are treated in which litigation does or is likely to occur.

Legal authority for public financial support. Wherever public money is involved litigation is a potential. Taxpayers are constantly scrutinizing the school program to determine for what purposes the school money is being expended. If public funds are provided for activities which some consider in conflict with constitutional and statutory provisions, and outside the intended purposes for which the schools are established, the legality of the expenditures could be, and often is, challenged. Therefore, Chapter 2 deals with the school district's authority to provide financial support for extracurricular activities.

Legality of restricting certain students from participation in extracurricular activities. Chapter 3 is concerned with the legality of school board regulations designed to discourage high school marriages and affiliation with secret societies, expecially fraternities.

Since student participation in extracurricular activities is usually optional, rather than mandatory, there are no court decisions of record involving requirements for participation therein. There are, however, a number of court cases growing out of the school board's denial of student participation in competitive athletics because of marriage or affiliation with secret societies. Chapter 3 refers to such cases.

Of the court cases concerning the issue, it will be noted that the majority of judicial rulings uphold the board's regulations designed to deter marriages or affiliation with fraternities by prohibiting offenders from participating in the extracurricular activities. It is significant to note, however, from the cases referred to in this volume, that the courts' rulings upholding boards of education in their restriction of student participation in extracurricular activities as deterrents or punitive measures are becuase of judicial reluctance to interfere with discretionary authority of school boards. Courts have repeatedly emphasized that they are not concerned with the wisdom or propriety of school board rules and regulations prescribing the qualifications for student participation in extracurricular activities.

Legal status of athletic associations. Very little research or writing has been done dealing with the legal authority of athletic associations to control certain phases of extracurricular activities. An attempt is made in Chapter 4 of this book to describe the legal status of these associations and their authority to make regulations affecting student participation in interscholastic athletic contests.

Surprisingly there has not been much litigation growing out of athletic associations mingling in the control of public school affairs. The authority of boards of education to control the entire school program, including extracurricular activities, is well recognized by students of school law. The legal authority of voluntary associations, without legal status, to control any aspect of school affairs is another matter.

Legality of teacher assignment for supervision of extracurricular activities. The legality and propriety of extra assignments to teachers without extra compensation has been an issue for a long time. In recent years, with the broadening of the school program to include additional student services and activities, the issue has become more pronounced. Obviously the teacher opposition to the extra assignments is more manifest during a period of teacher shortage and since tenure protection has become more widespread. After all, teachers are reluctant to place their positions in jeopardy by refusing to assume additional responsibilities even when they consider them unfair.

The cases referred to in Chapter 5 are those which have some bearing on so-called extracurricular activities. From the cases reported, it may be concluded that school boards, and even the courts, recognize the values inherent in extracurricular affairs. If it is assumed that the extracurricular activities have a legitimate place in the school program, it may be further assumed that the classroom teachers may be properly assigned the responsibility to supervise and administer certain aspects of them.

In a sense, an athletic coach may be regarded as a teacher of extracurricular activities. However, he could hardly be expected to supervise the entire student body or to aid in such matters as selling and collecting admission tickets at athletic contests. Most courts are likely to uphold the assignments of such duties to classroom teachers, providing the assignments are reasonable, nondiscriminatory, and related to the teachers' interests, abilities, and certification.

Tort liability as related to extracurricular activities. Tort liability of school districts and school personnel is an issue of vast proportions—far beyond the intended scope of this book. Chapter 6 deals only with tort liability cases involving extracurricular activities, and particularly interscholastic athletics.

In general a school district, because of its sovereign status, enjoys governmental immunity to liability for injuries sustained in educational activities. The same degree of immunity, however, does not apply to activities carried on by the school if they are of a proprietary rather than educational nature. The question, then, is whether or not extracurricular activities are educational and fall within the scope of governmental function. The question is particularly baffling where the activities are supported in part or entirely from fees, assessments, and gate receipts. According to some court decisions, a school district which charges fees for any purpose whatever jeopardizes its shield of immunity against tort liability.

Chapter 2

AUTHORITY OF SCHOOL DISTRICTS TO PROVIDE EXTRACURRICULAR FACILITIES

§ 2.1 Extracurricular financing in general

It is difficult to locate a school district which supports the total extracurricular program of its schools out of public funds. Conversely it is just as unusual to find a school district which does not, either directly or indirectly, support the extracurricular activities of its students to some degree. Because certain extracurricular activities are regarded by many persons as supplementary to the regular school program, the authority of school boards to give financial support to these activities has on occasions been challenged in the courts.

§ 2.2 Authority of school districts to expend public funds for extracurricular facilities

The authority of a school district to expend public funds for the construction of a stadium was upheld by the Supreme Court of Arizona in a case decided in 1927.[1]

The plaintiff, a taxpayer, charged that the Phoenix Union High School District could not, under the school laws of Arizona, issue bonds for the construction of a stadium. In the process of answering this question, the Supreme Court of

---

[1] Alexander v. Phillips, 31 Ariz 503, 254 Pac 1056 (1927).

Arizona had to determine whether a stadium was a school facility appropriate for school use and a facility in which educational pursuits were carried out.

Justifying the appropriateness of physical education and the facilities needed for it, the supreme court said:

> . . . [I]n the early days of our nation, it was not generally considered necessary for the public schools to attend to the physical education of the child. When 80 to 90 percent of our population was composed of farmers, it was universally thought the growing generation found an abundance . . . of physical training in the manifold duties of the home. But, with our modern industrial civilization, a great change has come over the land. At present over half our population is urban, with little or no chance for physical training for children in the home, and with the increase of human knowledge we are beginning to realize that the work of the farm and home even in the rural districts does not generally give a complete or properly rounded physical development. For this reason the new generation of educators has added to the mental education, which was all that was given by the public schools of the past, the proper training of the body, and a gymnasium is now accepted to be as properly a schoolhouse as is the chemical laboratory or the study hall.

Recognizing the valuable contribution of physical education to the total development of children, the court had to determine whether the expansion of the school program to include competitive sports for which a stadium was necessary was within the power of the school board under the laws of the state of Arizona. In regard to this question the court reasoned:

> That athletic games under proper supervision tend to the proper development of the body is a self evident fact. It is not always realized, however, that they have a most powerful and beneficial effect upon the development of character and morale. To use the one game of football as an illustration, the boy who makes a successful football player must necessarily learn self-control under the most trying circumstances, courage, both physical and moral, in

the face of strong opposition, sacrifice of individual ease for a community purpose, teamwork to the exclusion of individual glorification, and above all that "die in the last ditch" spirit which leads a man to do for a cause everything that is reasonably possible, and, when that is done, to achieve the impossible by sheer will power. The same is true to a greater or lesser degree of practically every athletic sport which is exhibited in a stadium.

It seems to us that, to hold things of this kind are less fitted for the ultimate purpose of our public schools, to wit, the making of good citizens, physically, mentally, and morally, than the study of algebra and Latin, is an absurdity. Competitive athletic games, therefore, from every standpoint, may properly be included in a public school curriculum.

The court concluded that the school board could legally construct a stadium because the school activities associated therewith were authorized by the laws of the state under the provision permitting "other special subjects" in addition to the regular curricular program.

The Court of Appeals of Kentucky, however, in a more recent case, failed to be pursuaded by the decision rendered by the Supreme Court of Arizona in *Alexander* v. *Phillips, supra,* in regard to the definition of a school building.[2]

A taxpayer who alleged that the board of education of Louisville could not repair a high school stadium by using moneys from a special fund for school buildings which was authorized by statute, brought suit for a declaration of rights. The court did not consider the question whether a stadium may be legally constructed by a board of education, but whether a stadium is a school building for which school building funds may be used for repair. Referring to and disagreeing with the Arizona court, Justice Cammack wrote:

The court apparently reasoned that, since a school house was a place for instruction, and since some athletic instruction took place in a stadium, a stadium was therefore a school house. This dubious logic was supported by

---

[2] Board of Ed. of Louisville v. Williams, 256 SW(2d) 29 (Ky, 1953).

a eulogy on the spiritual values of interscholastic athletic contests, of which the court took judicial notice. We think *Alexander* v. *Phillips* is not persuasive as to the intent of the Kentucky legislature in authorizing special taxes and special bond issues for "school buildings."

The Kentucky court did not declare that a school district could not build or repair a stadium; it only said that money from a special school buildings fund could not be used for such expenditures because, in its opinion, a stadium was not a school building.

Other courts, in general agreement with the Supreme Court of Arizona, have ruled that auditoriums, gymnasiums, and stadiums are school buildings [3] for the construction or repair of which a school district may legally issue bonds [4] or levy a special tax. [5] In an Oklahoma case [6] the court ruled that the residents of the school had a constitutional right to vote an extra tax levy to raise revenue for the erection of bleachers on a football field which the school district was authorized to maintain. More recently the attorney general of Ohio expressed that he was "... of the opinion that the board of education may place on the ballot a bond issue or a levy to make the various improvements to its athletic field." [7]

If land must be acquired for the construction of athletic facilities a school district has the authority to condemn land for such purposes. "The power of eminent domain is inherent in and essential to the existence of government. ..." [8] Several other courts reached similar conclusions by declaring

---

[3] Nichols v. Calhoun, 204 Miss 291, 37 S(2d) 313 (1948); Ranier v. Board of Ed. of Prestonsburg Independ. Sch. Dist. of Floyd County, 272 SW(2d) 577 (Ky, 1954).

[4] Woodson v. School Dist. No. 28, Kingman Co., 127 Kan 651, 274 Pac 728 (1929); McNair v. School Dist. No. 1 of Cascade Co., 87 Mont 423, 288 Pac 188 (1930); Moyer v. Board of Ed. of Sch. Dist. No. 186, 391 Ill 156, 62 NE(2d) 802 (1945); Nichols v. Calhoun, 204 Miss 291, 37 S(2d) 313 (1948).

[5] Ranier v. Board of Ed. of Prestonsburg Independ. Sch. Dist. of Floyd County, 272 SW(2d) 577 (Ky, 1954).

[6] Lowden v. Jefferson County Excise Bd., 190 Okla 276, 122 P(2d) 991 (1942).

[7] Opinions of the Attorney General of Ohio, 1961, No., 2479, pp. 528-32.

[8] Board of Ed. of Kanawha County v. Campbells Creek R. Co., 138 WVa 473, 76 SE(2d) 271 (1953).

that the acquision of land for athletic facilities could be obtained by the school board by invoking the power of eminent domain. [9]

§ 2.3   Cooperative financing of extracurricular facilities with noneducational agencies

In some instances municipalities and school districts operate in the financing of auditoriums and gymnasiums. A few cases have occurred in which the legal authority of a board of education to engage in such a project was challenged.

The city of Providence, Kentucky, adopted an ordinance providing for the issuance of bonds for the purpose of meeting the costs of constructing an auditorium-gymnasium to be used by the city and the school district. The payment of the interest on the retirement of the bonds was to be met by funds raised from rentals of the structure by both the city and the board of education.

The agreement, adopted in 1948, provided for a one-year lease to the board of education with the privilege of renewal, for which the school district would pay $3,500 per annum plus the cost of insurance and maintenance. The city would likewise have use of the building when such use did not conflict with school activities, for which it would pay $3,500 per annum into the bond and redemption fund. After seventeen years, and upon fulfillment of all agreements, the building and the land on which it was constructed was to become the property of the board of education at no cost to the school district.

When a declaratory judgment suit was brought to test the validity of the proposed bond issue, [10] the Court of Appeals of Kentucky, citing similar cases within its jurisdiction, [11] concluded that there was no legal objection to the proposed

[9] Sorenson v. Christiansen, 72 Wash 16, 129 Pac 577 (1913); Commissioner of Dist. of Columbia v. Shannon and Luchs Constr. Co., 57 AppDC 67, 17 F(2d) 219 (1927); Wey v. Ben Avon Borough Sch. Dist., 14 D&C 690 (Pa. 1930).
[10] Hill v. Providence, 307 Ky 537, 211 SW(2d) 846 (1948).
[11] Dodge v. Jefferson County Bd. of Ed., 289 Ky 1, 181 SW(2d) 406, (1944); Davis v. Board of Ed. of Newport, 260 Ky 294, 83 SW(2d) 34 (1934); McKinney v. Owensboro, 305 Ky 253, 203 SW(2d) 24 (1947); Dunn v. Murray, 306 Ky 426, 208 SW(2d) 309 (1948).

plan for financing the auditorium-gymnasium jointly by the city and the school board.

In a North Carolina case the state supreme court ruled that a school district could, under statutory provisions, convey an unimproved tract of land to the municipality in exchange for the use of a stadium to be constructed on the land. [12]

Statutory authority permitting a school district to purchase a recreation center jointly with a city or a county exists in the state of Kentucky. However, a school district was prohibited from purchasing a recreation center in another county for the benefit of the school children and for 4-H Club members. [13] The court of appeals declared that although the welfare of the pupils gave the board of education wide powers, this action was beyond its reasonable discretion and the tract of land which was purchased from the Tennessee Valley Authority for $2,500 had to be sold and the money restored to the school funds.

The question of the legality of the use of school tax funds for the construction of a stadium cooperatively by a county board of public instruction and a local nonprofit organization was submitted to the attorney general of Florida for his official opinion. [14] Answering this question in the affirmative, the attorney general said that the land on which the stadium was to be constructed could be deeded to the local Athletic Boosters Club, the organization financing the project, and that the school board could enter into an agreement with the club to pay $.50 per seat sold for each game played in the stadium until all the bonds were paid for. The attorney general also ruled that the local athletic association could take over maintenance for the duration of the lease. Dealing with a similar question in a companion opinion the attorney general reaffirmed the legality of boards of county commissioners and municipalities to construct auditoriums and swimming pools on municipal property for community and

---

[12] Boney v. Board of Trustees of Kingston Graded Schools, 229 NC 136, 48 SE(2d) 56 (1948).

[13] Wilson v. Graves County Bd. of Ed., 307 Ky 203, 210 SW(2d) 350 (1948).

[14] Biennial Report of the Attorney General of Florida, 1949-1950, No. 049-620, p. 290.

school use. [15] The attorney general did, however, stress the necessity for some permanent arrangement for the use of such a facility by the schools if public school funds were involved in its construction:

> . . .[I]t seems clear that the county board of public instruction cannot donate any. . . .funds for the construction of auditoriums and swimming pools by the county or a municipality, unless there be some permanent arrangement for the use of such auditoriums and swimming pools for educational purposes. . . .The use of such auditoriums and swiming pools by the schools would have to be something in addition to the general right of the public to use such facilities. The school authorities could not purchase rights and privileges that already belong to the school personnel and pupils.

§ 2.4   Expenditure of public funds for equipment and supplies for specific extracurricular activities

It is not uncommon for school districts to furnish equipment and supplies such as musical instruments, band uniforms, and athletic equipment for students participating in various extracurricular activities. Litigation has arisen in several states as a result of persons challenging the authority of boards of education to provide such items by expenditure of tax revenues.

On the authority of a Massachusetts statute which permitted school committees in cities and towns to expend money for the supervision of play and games on land under their control and for equipment needed therefor, [16] the school committee of Cambridge purchased various types of athletic clothing for a high school basketball team. The goods were acquired for the exclusive use by team members during practice and actual competition with other high school teams, some games of which were to be played away from Cambridge. The title of the goods was to be retained by the city, and any basketball player who became ineligible for

---

[15] Biennial Report of the Attorney General of Florida, 1949-1950, No. 049-475, pp. 308-9.

[16] Annotated Laws of Massachusetts, Vol. 2B, Chap. 71, Sec. 47.

team membership had to return his clothing to the school to be cleaned and reissued to some other eligible student.

An action of contract was brought against the city of Cambridge to recover the purchase price of these goods. [17] According to the Supreme Judicial Court of Massachusetts, the only authority, if any, permitting the school committee to purchase such goods to be loaned to the members of the basketball team was given by a statute which read in part: "[T]he committee shall, at the expense of the town, purchase textbooks and other school supplies, and under such regulations as to their care and custody as it may prescribe, shall loan them to the pupils free of charge." The court, quite aware that games and athletic exercises must be taught, was not convinced that athletic clothing was a part of the school supplies to be furnished for instruction: ". . . [T]o hold that athletic clothing is to be included as a part of school supplies required . . . [by law] to be furnished by the municipality, would be giving such an unusual meaning to the words 'school supplies' that we ought not to reach that conclusion unless the legislative purpose to include it clearly appears."

The court, restricting the meaning of school supplies to maps, charts, globes, and similar apparatus, ruled that the action of the school committee was beyond the express terms of the law and that the articles purchased were not school supplies within the meaning of the statute. An identical decision was rendered by the same court one year later when the authority of a school district to provide football apparel was challenged. [18]

The Supreme Court of Pennsylvania took a different view when deciding a similar case almost a decade later. [19] The opinion of this court is expressed in the words of Justice Stern:

> Physical education is as much a part of the school curriculum as are subjects of intellectual study, and athletic

---

[17] Brine v. Cambridge, 265 Mass 452, 164 NE 619 (1929).
[18] Wright and Ditson v. Boston, 265 Mass 452, 164 NE 619 (1930).
[19] Galloway v. School Dist. of Borough of Prospect Park, 331 Pa 48, 200 Atl 99 (1938).

supplies, therefore, are as "necessary for school use" as maps, globes, and similar objects. It is not the spirit of our public school system that only children with financial means to purchase their own supplies should have the opportunity of participating in school games and athletic sports.

The court did, however, express its concern about the number of pupils benefiting from the goods purchased:

> . . . [T]he extent to which athletic paraphernalia should be purchased for use merely by school teams playing in competitive sports is a question to be answered by school boards in the exercise of a cautious discretion, with special reference to the proportionate number of those who will receive the benefit of the supplies.

One year later, the Supreme Court of Oklahoma declared, in a 5-4 decision, that a school district could appropriate funds to purchase band uniforms. [20]

The Kay County Excise Board approved the annual budget of an independent school district, which included an appropriation to buy band uniforms. Contending that this appropriation for band uniforms was unauthorized and illegal, the Atchinson, Topeka, and Santa Fe Railway Company protested the excise board's approval of the school budget.

It was pointed out by the court that the state legislature conferred broad powers upon local school districts to conduct a public school system. Even in the absence of a statute expressly mentioning the purchase of band uniforms by school boards, such expenditures were within its general powers. The majority of the court said:

> [W]e hold that the appropriation was not for an unauthorized or illegal purpose. If this board, within all limits of levy, is able to pay all its other school operating expenses, and in addition thereto, is able to buy band uniforms, and obtains an appropriation therefor in reasonable

---

[20] Kay County Excise Bd. v. Atchinson, T., S. F. R. Co., 185 Okla 327, 91 P(2d) 1087 (1939).

amount, then expenditure therefor, within the specific appropriation, is legitimate and legal.

The views of the four dissenting justices were presented by Justice Gibson who wrote the dissenting opinion which read in part:

The members of the School Board are trustees for the taxpaying public in expending public funds in the maintenance and operation of the public schools. They must find authority in some statute before they can legally appropriate and spend such funds.

More recently the attorney general of Virginia in an official opinion expressed his belief that a school district has the discretionary power to purchase band uniforms if it so desires. [21] The attorney general issued this opinion in response to the question: May a county board of supervisors make a donation to a fund to be used for the purchase of uniforms for the local high school band? He said in part:

I am of the opinion that the provisions of the statute in question are not sufficiently broad to authorize the appropriation concerning which you inquire, nor am I aware of any other provision of the Virginia Code which expressly authorizes the governing bodies of the various counties of Virginia "to make gifts and donations" for the specific purpose . . . mention[ed]. However, I believe that it is within the area of permissible discretion for the County School Board. . . to determine whether or not the procurement of uniforms for the local high school band is reasonably incident to the operation of the public school program of the county, and if such determination is affirmatively made, I am constrained to believe that the Board of Supervisors. . . could properly appropriate funds to the school board to be expended for such purpose.

Although it is generally accepted that a board of education has a legal right to use tax revenues to purchase extracur-

---

[21] Opinions of the Attorney General and Report to the Governor of Virginia, July 1, 1961 – June 30, 1962, pp. 216-17.

ricular equipment, numerous school systems rely on the proceeds from gate receipts to purchase the needed supplies.

§ 2.5   Providing Transportation for extracurricular activities

Numerous school districts provide transportation for extracurricular groups, interscholastic athletics in particular. Although the subject is one of significance, few cases exist in which the legal implications of providing transportation for extracurricular activities is the subject of litigation.

The first applicable case came before the Supreme Court of Iowa in 1927. [22] Taxpayers initiated action against the school directors to enjoin expenditures for transportation to certain extracurricular activities. They contended that the school district was acting without authority because the buses were being used for purposes quite distinct from those specified in the statute. Upon receiving an adverse judgment in the district court, the school district appealed to the Supreme Court of Iowa. This court concluded that the school district could not provide transportation for extracurricular groups because ". . . the expenditure under complaint was unwarranted under the statute."

In a concurring opinion Justice DeGraff said:

> . . . [T]he school board, acting under its authority to transport pupils to and from school in the district, has no lawful right, and therefore no discretion, to use the means of transportation, to wit, motorbuses, for purposes entirely foreign to the subject-matter of the statute, and which have no relation to the management or operation of the school, or germane to any strictly school purpose. . . . The miscellaneous and incidental purposes disclosed by the instant record are but remotely connected with the operation of the school and in no wise connected with the transportation of children.

Some years later the Utah Supreme Court ruled that a school district could furnish transportation to those students

---

[22] Schmidt v. Blair, 203 Iowa 1016, 213 NW 593 (1927).

who were required to attend extracurricular functions, but not to those who were spectators. [23]

Suit was brought against the school district by the owner of a local opera house because the student activities association was providing competitive entertainment such as athletic games, dances, operas, and similar activities at school, to which the school district was providing transportation and paying all expenses except the wages of the bus drivers.

Assuming that extracurricular activities had a place in the curriculum, the court had to decide whether the board of education had the authority to furnish transportation to students and patrons to and from school at the expense of the school district for the purpose of attending such activities. Answering this question in the negative, the court said:

> . . . [T]here is no provision of law authorizing free transportation to students attending activities or entertainments where attendance is not compulsory. The expenditure of school funds for the purpose was properly enjoined. . . . There is testimony to the effect that students playing in the school band and taking part in dramatic performances and athletic contests are required by the school authority to attend the functions in which they personally participate. The other students may attend such performances at their option, and, when they do attend, it is merely as spectators, and not because their attendance is required. The decree should not enjoin the furnishing of free transportation to students whose attendance is required after school hours at school activities. It of course follows that the board may not, at any expense to the district, or by use of school property, furnish free transportation to the patrons of entertainments, games, or other activities.

The Supreme Court of Kansas ruled that a school board could transport pupils outside the district only if a contract to do so existed. [24] In the absence of such a contract, as is

---

[23] Beard v. Board of Ed. of North Summit Sch. Dist., 81 Utah 51, 16 P(2d) 900 (1932).

[24] Carothers v. Board of Ed. of Florence, 153 Kan 126, 109 P(2d) 63 (1941).

the case with most extracurricular activities, transportation was prohibited.

In a more recent case in North Carolina, the supreme court reasoned that since school bands and athletic teams are under the control of school authorities, ". . . the board [of education] controlling such activities would have the inherent right to contract for such transportation as might be necessary to transport its athletic teams and its bands to and from such events as have been scheduled under the[ir] supervision. . . ."[25] The court also ruled that such transportation would not come under the control of the Bus Act of 1949, which provides for exempting those persons supervised by school authorities, thus recognizing the legality of a school district to provide transportation for bands and athletic teams.

Because of the absence of court decisions, in some states the question of the legality of providing transportation to extracurricular activities has been submitted to the various attorneys general for an official opinion. The attorney general of California said that school districts could provide buses but could not assume the expense of transporting school bands to reviews and contests,[26] and more recently the attorney general of Indiana had the following to say about the transportation of 4-H Club members to various activities:[27]

> . . . I am of the opinion no authority is given by statute for the use of school buses to transport 4-H Club members and leaders to meetings and events educational in nature, even though approved by the local school administrators, unless it is a "school function". . . .

In the absence of a sufficient number of court cases it is impossible to arrive at a definite legal principle in regard to a school district's authority to expend tax funds for the trans-

---

[25] State ex rel. North Carolina Util. Comm. v. McKinnon, 254 NC 1, 118 SE(2d) 134 (1961).

[26] Opinions of the Attorney General of California, January-June 1947, Vol. 9, No. 47-38, pp. 151-52.

[27] Opinions of the Attorney General of Indiana, 1962, No. 46, pp. 245-47.

portation of extracurricular groups. Unless there are definite statutes permitting such transportation or unless a school district is specifically authorized to carry out such activities as part of its total school program, there arises the question of whether a school district can legally expend public funds for the transportation of pupils to and from extracurricular events. The courts and the attorneys general of several states are not completely convinced that a school board can assume the total expense of transportation. There does seem to be a general agreement that school buses may be used for extracurricular activities but that school districts cannot assume the expense of operating them. Only after further litigation will it be possible to arrive at a definite legal principle in regard to this problem.

§ 2.6   Use of school facilities for extracurricular events

Sometimes taxpayers, because of vested interests or because of their opposition to various extracurricular activities, have attempted to prohibit school districts from using their buildings for certain extracurricular events.

The Supreme Court of Utah rendered a judgment favorable to a board of education when an owner of a competing opera house sought an injunction against the school district to enjoin it from allowing the high school building to be used for the holding of public and private dances, shows, dramatics, motion pictures, operas, basketball games, and other kinds of entertainment not directly connected with the curriculum and for which admission was charged.[28]

The plaintiff contended that the use of a tax-exempt, tax-supported institution to compete with a taxpayer was unfair competition. The court did not agree. Ruling that there was no ground for complaint so long as a school was used for the purposes authorized by law, the court said:

That the student body organization and proper activities thereof are part of the educational system of the district we think admits of no doubt. The scope of its activity, as

---

[28] Beard v. Board of Ed. of North Summit Sch. Dist., 81 Utah 51, 16 P(2d) 900 (1932).

indicated by the constitution, shows a purpose closely related to the school curriculum, although not required thereby, and is certainly within what is now regarded by all educators as a modern educational system.

....

The activities referred to in the student body constitution are clearly educational and a part of an enlarged modern educational program. . . .

In response to the complaint that the extracurricular activities were of a commercial nature which constituted unfair competition for a local opera house, the court had the following comment:

. . . [E]xtracurricular activities are a proper and necessary part of our educational system, and hence cannot be considered as carried on for commercial purposes. What is done for the student body for reasons which concern the educational welfare of the students cannot be said. . . to be done for commercial purposes.

Several other courts have also held that resident taxpayers cannot enjoin a school board from permitting the use of its buildings for athletic contests, dances, and other social activities.[29]

§ 2.7 Legal problems of profit-making

Sometimes the profit-making activities of a school board in relation to its extracurricular activities program result in legal problems. Litigation has occurred as a result of both direct profits, such as gate receipts and broadcast fees derived from extracurricular events themselves, and indirect profits realized by the renting or leasing of extracurricular facilities.

When a dispute arose between a school district and two broadcasting companies which both claimed a right to broadcast athletic events, the court of civil appeals of Texas ruled that a school district has the exclusive control of its premises

---

[29] Brooks v. Elder, 108 Neb 761, 189 NW 284 (1922); Merryman v. School Dist. No. 16, 43 Wyo 376, 5 P(2d) 267 (1931).

and the right to make a profit for its own benefit.[30] The court, ruling in favor of the school district and the broadcasting company it had chosen to broadcast its games, said in part:

> . . . [E]ven though the District is a quasi-municipal corporation, it has a right to seek to make a profit out of the games played on its premises; the profit, of course, to go for the benefit of the District. We can see no good reason why it should not have the same freedom of action as a private person or corporation putting on the games. The district owns the field and the grandstand. The appealing defendants have no right, against the will of the District, to enter upon its field and pursue a business activity thereon for profit.

> . . . The duty imposed by the contract in question on KRIG was to broadcast all games. It is a reasonable inference that the broadcasting of the games would stimulate interest therein and promote the attendance at future games. In making this contract, the School Board was not seeking to arbitrarily benefit KRIG, but furthering the interest of the District, by which contract it was assured that the games would be broadcast.

A school district, in the opinion of the court, has exclusive control over its property and no corporation may legally carry on a business on school premises against the will of the board of education.

In a more recent case the Supreme Court of Colorado ruled that a school district could charge a private radio station a fee for the privilege of broadcasting football games. [31]

If a school district does not spend all of the funds received from extracurricular activities for educational purposes as defined by the court, it might be required to pay sales tax on the money received. The Supreme Court of Kansas ruled that

---

[30] Southwestern Broadcasting Co. v. Oil Center Broadcasting Co., 210 SW(2d) 230 (Tex, 1947).

[31] Colorado High School Activities Assn. v. Uncompahgre Broadcasting Co., 300 P(2d) 968 (Colo, 1956).

when receipts for admission to extracurricular events are not entirely expended for education purposes a school is not entitled to exemption from taxation under the state sales tax statute. [32]

The State Tax Commission sought a mandamus to compel a board of education to register and collect taxes as required by the state law. The plaintiffs contended that profits received by school organizations through the sale of admission tickets, sweaters, and soft drinks were subject to taxation because these endeavors were not of an educational nature.

The court said that admission charges did not make the extracurricular activities noneducational, but that the school board was not exempt from paying taxes on admissions unless the entire amount of money received was used for educational purposes. Aware of the difficulty of determining a line of demarcation between those activities which clearly fall within the "educational" category and those which do not, the majority of the court concluded:

> . . . [W]e are clear the purchases of athletic goods, confectionery, and soda pop for resale were not expenditures for educational purposes. And in connection with the Girl Reserves and Hi-Y activities, we have no difficulty in determining that using a part of its funds for the purpose of defraying the expenses of parties and picnics and for the purchase of gifts for some unmentioned recipient lacks much of being an educational purpose, and the same may be said concerning the use of activity funds for the purpose of an all school party.

Disagreeing with the majority of the court, Justic Smith in his dissenting opinion said:

> I hold that once it is admitted that these activities are educational, then one is led inevitably to the conclusion that any money expended for a purpose incidental to these activities is expended for an educational purpose.

---

[32] State Tax Comm. v. Board of Ed. of Holton, 146 Kan 722, 73 P(2d) 49 (1937).

Defending the activities of school parties and picnics as being of educational value Justice Smith continued:

The[se] organizations are part of any up-to-date school program. the parties given by such organizations are in many cases the only social intercourse available to students.

This sort of thing has become as much a part of the training given a student as the reading, writing, and arithmetic of the classroom. Who are we to say that the expenditure of money for putting on such a party or picnic is not the expenditure of it for educational purposes? It is all done under the supervision of the faculty of the various schools. The benefits all flow to students participating, and any student wishing to join and take part may do so.

Sometimes disputes involving the authority of a school district to rent or lease athletic facilities to other than school groups culminates in litigation. In one such case the court of civil appeals of Texas ruled that a board of education could permit a local booster club to use a portion of the school premises for baseball during the summer vacation.[33]

The Royce Independent School District had a contract with the Royce Booster Club to permit the club to use a portion of the school campus for baseball games. The plaintiffs brough suit for an injunction to prohibit the school board from honoring the contract because, as they contended, the board of education had no authority to use or rent public school property for other than educational purposes.

The court of civil appeals, in rendering a judgment favorable to the school district, said in part:

The primary object in granting the privilege to the Royce Booster Club to use its school grounds as a place to play baseball is to subserve a public purpose, and not to promote some private end. And it clearly appears that such incidental use of the grounds could in no way impair the

---

33 Royce Independ. Sch. Dist. v. Reinhardt, 159 SW 1010 (Tex, 1913).

school buildings, or interfere in any wise with the orderly and successful conduct of the school.

The contract under consideration permits the use of the school grounds only during the period of time intervening between the close of the school in the spring and the beginning of the term in the following fall, and will result in quite a financial advantage to the school district. It may be true that the use to which the grounds will be put under the contract is not actually necessary for the promotion of the school, yet, as it will not impede or interfere with its progress, or tend to injure the school property, and will be used at a time when the grounds are not needed and will not be used by the school, such use is not so inconsistent with the purpose to which the property has been dedicated or set apart as renders the contract permitting it illegal or unauthorized. In other words, we think the contract between the trustees of the Royce independent school district and the Royce Booster Club, whereby said trustees lease to said club a portion of its unused school campus for the purpose of playing baseball thereon during vacation, . . . is not ultra vires or unauthorized.

Similarly, the Supreme Court of Idaho ruled that the leasing of a public school athletic field to a private ball club was not invalid as lending credit of the school district to aid private objectives. [34]

In a more recent case, the Supreme Court of South Carolina declared void a similar lease agreement because the private ball club, in addition to being a public nuisance, interfered with school activities.[35]

The court, concluding that the private ball club interfered with the educational pursuits of the school, expressed its views as follows:

. . . [W]e think that it is implicit in the evidence that there is . . . interference [with school activities]. Only one athletic field is owned by the Lake City High School for the use of the boys and girls who attend the school.

[34] Hansen v. Independent Sch. Dist. No. 1 in Nez Perce County, 61 Idaho 109, 98 P(2d) 959 (1940).

[35] Carter v. Lake City Baseball Club, 218 SC 255, 62 SE(2d) 470 (1950).

The professional ballplayers on the Lake City Baseball Club take possession of the baseball field early in April for their practice, looking toward the beginning of their schedule of games; and their playing season opens on May 2nd. The school term ends June 1st, so that during most of April and all of May of the school session, the use of this field is practically denied to the school children.

Since the private ball club was given free and unimpeded use of the high school athletic field during a portion of the school year the court ruled that " . . . the school trustees had no power to lease or permit the use of the school athletic field for the playing of professional or semi-professional baseball during the school term . . . and that the lease . . . [was] null and void."

A school district may engage in profit-making ventures in connection with extracurricular activities so long as such enterprises do not interfere with the regular school program. However, a school district which does make profits may waive its sovereign immunity for tort liability by pursuing activities which are not totally governmental. This problem is dealt with in Chapter 6.

§ 2.8   Supervision of extracurricular funds

Extracurricular activities are rarely entirely subsidized by the board of education; it is therefore necessary for extracurricular groups to raise money either through gate receipts or by conducting various other fund-raising endeavors. Since these moneys are not tax revenues the question frequently arises as to whether they are public or nonpublic funds. If such moneys are public funds they come under the custody of the school board, through which approval for all financial transactions must be obtained. Hamilton stressed the point that extracurricular funds are no different than other school funds: "It is quite generally assumed by school people that special funds are of a character different from those raised by taxation, fines, forfeitures, and grants, hence are subject to different controls. . . . [S]uch is not the case . . ."[36]

36 R. R. Hamilton, "The Legal Status, Control and Use of Athletic and Other Extra-curricular Funds," The Bi-Weekly School Law Letter, II (September 18, 1952), p. 57.

The first significant case in which the subject of litigation was the supervision of extracurricular funds occurred in Pennsylvania in 1942.[37] The German Township School Directors created an athletic control board, on the theory that all extracurricular activities could be entirely segregated from the supervision of the board of education as a board. They were under the impression that they could delegate all jurisdication over extracurricular activities and the handling of finances incident to such management to an appointed athletic control board, some members of which were members of the board of directors.

The board of directors insisted that the purchase of athletic equipment and band uniforms and the expenditure of proceeds from athletic and band activities was within the authority of the athletic control board without any supervision from the board of education as a whole. Following this line of reasoning, the athletic control board deposited the proceeds of athletic games in a local bank and drew checks against the account in payment of bills without regard to the provisions in the school code requiring school board approval for such payments. Under this arrangment none of the extracurricular funds ever reached the school treasury, and the account was never audited by the township auditors.

By the time suit was filed against the school directors for their removal because of irregularities in financial management, one charge of which was directed at the supervision of extracurricular funds, the athletic control board had already authorized the purchase of athlctic supplies and equipment and band uniforms costing $965.30 and $1,421.20, respectively.

In defending its action to delegate the duty of supervision and control of all extracurricular activities to the athletic control board, the board of directors cited a portion of the school code which provided for school boards to " . . . prescribe, adopt, and enforce such reasonable rules and regulations. . ." as are required for the management of extracurricular activities. Although the school code permitted the board of education to make reasonable rules and regula-

[37] In re German Tp. School Directors, 46 D&C 562 (Pa, 1942).

tions governing extracurricular activities, it granted no authority to divorce extracurricular activities from the curricular program of the school. The court said:

> The language of this section in no sense serves to divorce the athletic and musical organizations of the high school from the other departments of the public schools. It cannot be construed as clothing a board of athletic control with supreme authority over the finances required to conduct these departments. The members of the band, who receive instructions in playing the various instruments used in such an organization, and who take part in the varied exercises that take place on the football field, particularly between the halves of the game, are as much a part of the student body as are those who specialize in intellectual achievements.
>
> The comparatively small number of athletically inclined boys who survive the rigors of the training period and carry the colors of the school on the football field are not to be regarded as separate from the great body of pupils in the public schools who are not able, or do not choose, to participate in this line of endeavor.
>
> If this select few acquiring such special skill in the playing of the game of football, and the relatively small number of pupils who comprise the high school band, by their combined efforts are able to attract large crowds of spectators who are willing to pay substantial admission prices for the entertainment furnished, such students and such activities may not be regarded as a separate institution, subject only to the supervision of the athletic board of control. They constitute a unit or department of the entire school system. They receive no part of the prices of admission. They do not perform for the athletic board of control. They carry on for [their] alma mater. The proceeds of these activities belong to the board of school directors and must be accounted for in the same manner that other funds of the school district are accounted for.

The court pointed out that the athletic control board had no greater powers and duties than a board of education committee, but that it could continue to exist so long as ". . . all moneys received . . . and all expenditures . . . [were] reported to and approved by the board of directors as a board."

Because of the absence of ". . . any contemplation or receipt of profit by any director from the manner in which the athletic finances were handled" the court did not remove from office any of the school directors. They were absolved from any willful failure to comply with the mandatory provisions of the school code.

Several years later another Pennsylvania court came to a similar conclusion by ruling that school activities funds must be deposited in the official school account and must be handled as regular public funds.[38]

A school district, in addition to its regular official account, had an activities account in a local bank. The supervising principal of the school district, under the control of the school board, had the sole right to withdraw funds therefrom.

When a dispute arose in relation to the auditing of the activities account, the school authorities sought a court determination of the question: Is an activities account subject to audit even though no tax money is deposited in it? The court answered this question in the affirmative, by ruling that all money raised through extracurricular activities becomes a part of the official school account because it is raised through the aid of the school district's investment: buildings, equipment, and personnel.

The court, aware of the possibility that some school districts might not, directly or indirectly, furnish financial support for extracurricular activities, said in part:

> . . . [I]t is certainly true that, if a school district operates and expends tax money for the acquisition, maintenance or lighting of the playing field, or for the services of a coach, the admissions charged result from the use of public property and from the expenditure of tax monies and are the property of the school district, must go into

---

[38] Petition of Auditors of Hatfield Twp. Sch. Dist., 161 PaSuper 388, 54 A(2d) 833 (1947).

the official account of the treasurer thereof, and are subject to audit.

The court pointed out that the same principle would be applicable to money raised by music, drama, or other extracurricular activities conducted through the use of school facilities or personnel either directly or indirectly.

A Kentucky court recognized the authority of a board of education to control activities funds, yet regarded its duty to do so as different from its supervision of tax-derived income. [39]

A principal and his high school athletic coach purchased athletic equipment, and, because the purchase was made with its full knowledge, the board of education could not deny liability for the debt. The court held that the board of education could not claim immunity for the debt incurred because through its supervision of the activities fund it acted in a quasi-private manner. The court said in part:

> It is our belief [that] the board in its general supervision of the activities fund has not acted in a governmental capacity, but rather in a quasi-private proprietary manner. It is undenied [that] the monies in the fund are not tax-derived income, so that the legal precepts that ordinarily apply to revenue obtained by taxation for educational purposes do not apply. This being true, the board cannot claim immunity as to the liability of the activities fund for the debts sued on that it could of the income sought to be subjected came through tax channels.

In a recent Kentucky case a member of a board of education and principal stockholder of a soft drink bottling company vacated his position by selling soft drinks to schools of his district even though the profits were used for school athletic supplies, repairs of band equipment, and class trips. [40]

The attorney general of Kentucky brought suit against a school board member for engaging in what he regarded as

---

[39] Board of Ed. of Anderson County v. Calvert, 321 SW(2d) 413 (Ky, 1959).
[40] Commonwealth of Ky. ex rel. Breckinridge v. Collins, 379 SW(2d) 436 (Ky, 1964).

improper business transactions with the school district. Upon receiving an adverse judgment in the circuit court of Letcher County, the attorney general appealed the case to the Court of Appeals of Kentucky. He contended that the profits from the sale of soft drinks were school funds used to promote public education and should come within the supervisory control of the board of education. The appellee argued that these profits were not school funds because they were kept separate and apart from tax revenue and there were no sales or payments which involved the school board or the school funds. He also contended that these funds, raised by pupils from school projects, belonged to the various class organizations.

The court concluded, by citing *Anderson County* v. *Calvert, supra*, that, by legislative intent, activity funds are school funds over which the school board has full control. Thus the school board member, through his actions, violated the law and in so doing vacated his position.

In a 1961 South Carolina case the court recognized the existence of school funds not administered either directly or indirectly by the board of education. [41]

Funds derived from extracurricular activities were entrusted to the supervising principal of a school district. Neither the raising nor the disbursement of this money was supervised by the board of trustees. The entire undertaking was conducted through the voluntary endeavors of the pupils and teachers.

Legal action was initiated by taxpayers and parents against the principal to require him to account for the funds. The plaintiffs also contended that the maintenance of this fund by the school authorities was not authorized by law and was therefore beyond their lawful powers.

The court of common pleas of Jasper County dismissed the case, but upon appeal the Supreme Court of South Carolina modified the lower court's ruling. The supreme court declared that the principal had " . . . the duty of rendering a full and accurate accounting of his administration . . . [of extracurricular funds], showing a complete

---

[41] Betterson v. Stewart, 238 SC 574, 121 SE(2d) 102 (1961).

statement of his receipts, disbursements, and any balance
remaining." But in regard to the authority of the board of
trustees to maintain such a fund the court said:

> The record shows that the fund in question was not
> raised or maintained by the school authorities but was
> purely a voluntary endeavor on the part of patrons,
> teachers, and pupils of the school for the purpose of pro-
> moting the welfare of the school and its students. Since
> the fund in question was not raised or administered, either
> directly or indirectly, by the Board of Trustees, the ques-
> tion of whether they have such power is not an issue and
> need not be considered.

§ 2.9   Summary

Most school districts support extracurricular activities, at
least in part, by expending tax-derived funds, and their
authority to do so has been challenged by taxpayers who
allege that it is illegal to use public revenues to finance extracurricular activities because they are not part of the regular
school program.

In a significant case which occurred in 1927, the Supreme
Court of Arizona declared that competitive sports were properly included in the school curriculum and that the school
district had the authority to issue bonds for the construction
of a stadium.[42] Failing to be persuaded by the Supreme
Court of Arizona, a Kentucky court ruled that a school district did not have the authority to use money in a special
school building fund to repair a stadium.[43] The court, however, did not say that the board of education could not build
and maintain a stadium; it only ruled that a stadium was not
a school building and that money from a special school buildings fund could not be used for repairing it. Most courts,
rendering decisions in agreement with the Supreme Court of
Arizona, have upheld the authority of school districts to expend public funds for the construction and maintenance of
auditoriums, gymnasiums, and stadiums.[44] The courts have

[42] Alexander v. Phillips, 31 Ariz 503, 254 Pac 1056 (1927).
[43] Board of Ed. of Louisville v. Williams, 256 SW(2d) 29 (Ky, 1953).
[44] Woodson v. School Dist. No. 28, Kingman Co., 127 Kan 651, 274 Pac 728
(1929); McNair v. School Dist. No. 1 of Cascade Co., 87 Mont 423, 288 Pac 188

also held that boards of education may invoke their power of eminent domain to acquire land on which to construct athletic facilities. [45]

Occasionally school districts and municipalities cooperate in financing the construction of auditoriums, gymnasiums, stadiums, and swimming pools. The courts have generally upheld such cooperative arrangements; [46] however, the Court of Appeals of Kentucky declared that a school district could not purchase a recreation center in another county under a statute permitting a school district to purchase jointly with a city or county a recreation center for use by its pupils. [47]

As a rule, school boards furnish supplies to be used by students participating in extracurricular activities. In two decisions rendered by the Supreme Judicial Court of Massachusetts, the authority of a school district to provide apparel for basketball and football teams was stricken down, [48] but two other courts declared that similar expenditures were legitimate and within the power of the school board. [49]

It is not uncommon for school districts to expend public funds in order to provide transportation for extracurricular groups, yet few cases pertaining to the subject have reached the appellate courts. Of the cases to come before the courts, the number is too few and the opinions too varied to arrive at

(1930); Lowden v. Jefferson County Excise Bd., 190 Okla 276, 122 P(2d) 991 (1942); Moyer v. Board of Ed. of Sch. Dist. No. 186, 391 Ill 156, 62 NE(2d) 802 (1945); Nichols v. Calhoun, 204 Miss 291, 37 S(2d) 313 (1948); Ranier v. Board of Ed. of Prestonsburg Independ. Sch. Dist. of Floyd Co., 272 SW(2d) 577 (Ky, 1954). See also Opinions of the Attorney General of Ohio, 1961 No. 2479, pp. 528-32.

[45] Sorenson v. Christianson, 72 Wash 16, 129 Pac 577 (1913); Commissioner of Dist. of Columbia v. Shannon and Luchs Constr. Co., 57 AppDC 67, 17 F(2d) 219 (1927); Wey v. Ben Avon Borough Sch. Dist., 14 D&C 690 (Pa, 1930).

[46] Hill v. Providence, 307 Ky 537, 211 SW(2d) 846 (1948); Boney v. Board of Trustees of Kingston Graded Schools, 229 NC 136, 48 SE(2d) 56 (1948). See also Biennial Report of the Attorney General of Florida, 1949-1959, No. 049-620, p. 290 and No. 049-475, pp. 308-09.

[47] Wilson v. Graves County Bd. of Ed., 307 Ky 203, 210 SW(2d) 350 (1948).

[48] Brine v. Cambridge, 265 Mass 452, 164 NE 619 (1929); Wright and Ditson v. Boston, 265 Mass 452, 164 NE 619 (1930).

[49] Galloway v. School Dist. of Borough of Prospect Park, 331 Pa 48, 200 Atl 99 (1938); Kay County Excise Bd. v. Atchinson, T, & S F R Co., 185 Okla 327, 91 P(2d) 1087 (1939). See also Opinions of the Attorney General and Report to the Governor of Virginia, July 1, 1961 – June 30, 1961, pp. 216-17.

a definite legal principle regarding this phase of extra-curricular activities.

The Supreme Court of Iowa ruled that a school district could not provide transportation for extracurricular groups because the expenditure was unwarranted under the school code.[50] In the state of Utah the supreme court declared that a board of education could provide transportation for students who were required to attend extracurricular events, but not for spectators.[51] And boards of education in Kansas, according to a decision of the supreme court of that state, were not permitted to transport students outside of the school district unless a contract to do so existed.[52] In a more recent case, the Supreme Court of North Carolina ruled that boards of education had the inherent right to contract for the necessary transportation for athletic teams and school bands.[53] Because of the absence of court cases, some attorneys general have been requested to issue official opinions in regard to the legality of providing transportation of pupils to extracurricular events. The attorney general of California declared that school districts could use school buses to transport school bands to reviews and contests, but that they could not assume the expense of operating the buses.[54] The attorney general of Indiana more recently stated in an official opinion that a board of education had no authority to use its buses to transport 4-H Club members to activities unless such events were school functions.[55]

Although some taxpayers have attempted to prohibit school districts from using their buildings for certain extra-curricular events, the courts have held that they cannot enjoin a school board from using its buildings for athletic contests, dances, and other social activities.[56]

[50] Schmidt v. Blair, 203 Iowa 1016, 213 NW 593 (1927).

[51] Beard v. Board of Ed. of North Summit Sch. Dist., 81 Utah 51, 16 P(2d) 900 (1932).

[52] Carothers v. Board of Ed. of Florence, 153 Kan 126, 109 P(2d) 63 (1941).

[53] State ex rel. North Carolina Util. Comm. v. McKinnon, 254 NC 1, 188 SE(2d) 134 (1961).

[54] Opinions of the Attorney General of California, January-June 1947, Vol. 9, No. 47-38, pp. 151-52.

[55] Opinions of the Attorney General of Indiana, 1962, No. 46, pp. 245-47.

[56] Brooks v. Elder, 108 Neb 761, 189 NW 284 (1922); Merryman v. School

School districts sometimes encounter the problem of becoming involved in lawsuits as a result of profit-making ventures associated with extracurricular activities, although in most cases the courts decide in their favor. But one court ruled that unless all funds received from extracurricular activities were used for educational purposes, the school district would be required to pay state sales tax on the money received.[57]

The right of boards of education to charge a radio station fees for broadcasting football games has been upheld by the courts.[58] Likewise, the courts have ruled that a school district may rent its athletic facilities to private athletic groups[59] so long as the contract can be fulfilled without interfering with school activities.[60]

Since proceeds raised in the conduct of extracurricular activities are not tax revenues, the question has arisen as to whether they are public funds which come under the custody of the board of education. Several courts have ruled that proceeds of extracurricular activities are public funds and must be accounted for in the same manner as other school district funds.[61] However, a Kentucky court recognized the authority of a board of education to control activity funds, yet regarded its duty to do so as quasi-private, which waived the school district's governmental immunity as to the liability in regard to debts incurred by those in charge of the activities funds.[62] Although it is generally accepted that extracur-

---

Dist. No. 16, 43 Wyo 376, 5 P(2d) 267 (1931); Beard v. Board of Ed. of North Summit Sch. Dist., 81 Utah 51, 16 P(2d) 900 (1932).

[57] State Tax Comm. v. Board of Ed. of Holton, 146 Kan 722, 73 P(2d) 49 (1937).

[58] Southwestern Broadcasting Co. v. Oil Center Broadcasting Co., 210 SW(2d) 230 (Tex, 1947); Colorado High School Activities Assn. v. Uncompahgre Broadcasting Co., 300 P(2d) 968 (Colo, 1956).

[59] Royce Independ. Sch. Dist. v. Reinhardt, 159 SW 1010 (Tex, 1913); Hansen v. Independent Sch. Dist. No. 1 in Nez Perce County, 61 Idaho 109, 98 P(2d) 959 (1940).

[60] Carter v. Lake City Baseball Club, 218 SC 255, 62 SE(2d) 470 (1950).

[61] In re German Tp. Sch. Directors, 46 D&C 562 (Pa, 1942); Petition of Auditors of Hatfield Tp. Sch. Dist., 161 PaSuper 388, 54 A(2d) 833 (1947).

[62] Board of Ed. of Anderson County v. Calvert, 321 SW(2d) 413 (Ky, 1959). See also Commonwealth of Ky. ex rel. Breckinridge v. Collins, 379 SW(2d) 436 (Ky, 1964).

ricular funds belong to the school district and should be handled accordingly, the Supreme Court of South Carolina recognized the existence of extracurricular funds not administered either directly or indirectly by the board of education.[63]

---

63 Betterson v. Stewart, 238 SC 574, 121 SE(2d) 102 (1961).

Chapter 3

LEGALITY OF RULES AND REGULATIONS CONCERNING THE PARTICIPATION OF PUBLIC SCHOOL PUPILS IN EXTRACURRICULAR ACTIVITIES

§ 3.1   Responsibility of states as to extracurricular activities

Most state constitutions provide for a *uniform* system of public schools open to all the children of the state. The Colorado constitution is typical in this respect: "The general assembly shall . . . provide for the establishment and maintenance of a thorough and uniform system of free public schools throughout the state, wherein all residents of the state, between the ages of six and twenty-one, may be educated gratuitously." [1]

Because the various school systems of a state have different programs of instruction and requirements, the question sometimes arises as to what constitutes a uniform system of public schools.

Uniformity does not mean identity, a dead level sameness, a complete lack of distinction. Uniformity does not preclude classification. It is not necessary that every school and every district should have exactly the same course of study . . . . Neither is it necessary that all the children of the state be given exactly the same educational privileges. [2]

---

[1] Constitution of Colorado, Article X, Section 2.
[2] Newton Edwards, The Courts and the Public Schools. Chicago: The University of Chicago Press, 1955, p. 32.

"While most people regard the public schools as the means of great personal advantage to the pupils, the fact is too often overlooked that they are governmental means of protecting the state from the consequences of an ignorant and incompetent citizenry." [3] The welfare of society requires the state to exert its sovereign authority to provide its youth with the privilege of receiving an education. [4] "This privilege is granted, and is to be enjoyed, upon such terms and under such reasonable conditions and restrictions as the law-making power, within constitutional limits, may see fit to impose. . . ." [5]

The state has not only the power but also the responsibility to establish laws and regulations for the efficient government of the public schools. As a result of the exercise of this power, particularly through its local representatives, the boards of education, the state exerts a degree of control over the personal freedom of the individual pupils in the public schools.

Although an individual sacrifices a degree of his freedom for the welfare of society, a state may not enforce rules and regulations which violate personal liberties guaranteed by the United States Constitution. For example, in the area of civil rights a board of education has no legal grounds for requiring or encouraging racial discrimination in extracurricular activities. The United States Court of Appeals, Fifth Circuit rule that [6]

. . . School officials should not discourage Negro children from enrolling in white schools, directly or indirectly, as for example, by advising them that they would not be permitted to engage or would (not) want to engage in school activities, athletics, the band, clubs, school plays.

---

[3] Fogg v. Board of Ed. of Union Sch. Dist. of Littleton, 76 NH 296, 82 Atl 173 (1912).

[4] Bissell v. Davison, 65 Conn 183, 32 Atl 348 (1894); State v. Bailey, 157 Ind 324, 61 NE 730 (1901).

[5] Ibid.

[6] United States v. Jefferson County Board of Education, 372 F(2d) 836 (1966).

Reaffirming what was stated in one of its earlier opinions, the Fifth Circuit Court of Appeals said: [7]

> . . . (T)here should be no segregation or discrimination in services, facilities, activities, and programs that may be conducted or sponsored by, or affiliated with, the school in which a student is enrolled.

The question of concern in this chapter is the right of a state, whose constitution provides for a "uniform" system of public schools, to prohibit, either by action of its legislature or its boards of education, the participation of pupils in various extracurricular activities.

§ 3.2 Authority of school officials to regulate extracurricular organizations

A Massachusetts statute provides for local control over various school organizations: "The [school] committee may supervise and control all athletic and other organizations composed of public school pupils and bearing the school name or organized in connection therewith." [8] Under the authority of this statute, a local school committee passed a resolution requiring the officers of unapproved secret organizations to file with the principal the following information:

1. Name of the organization
2. Lists of all student members
3. Dates and places of all meetings
4. Programs
5. Dates and places of all house parties and other gatherings whether occurring during school year or over short vacations

When the authority of the school committee to make such a regulation was challenged, the Supreme Judicial Court of Massachusetts rendered a judgment favorable to the school officials. [9] The court said that the school authorities had the

---

7 Singleton v. Jackson Municipal Separate School District, 355 F(2d) 865 (1966).

8 Annotated Laws of Massachusetts, Vol. 2B, Chap. 71, Sec. 47.

9 Antell v. Stokes, 287 Mass 103, 191 NE 407 (1934).

power to control athletic organizations under the laws of Massachusetts and that this power " . . . include[d] other organizations as well as those purely athletic. The legislative intent to cede power embracing every kind of such organization could hardly be more clear."

An Oregon board of education passed a resolution specifying the conditions under which school clubs could be organized. All organizations of pupils had to be approved by the central school administration; upon submission of the following information all approved organizations received a charter:

1. Sponsoring group
2. An adult advisor or advisors to be in charge of the organization
3. A constitution
4. The purposes of the organization and the standards upon which membership shall be based
5. A list of officers and members
6. A copy of any ceremonial or initiation
7. . . . [A] statement that the organization will not pledge any of its members to secrecy as to ritual, purpose, activities, or membership

Eighteen rules were issued by the school board for the government of chartered clubs. It was one of these rules that was challenged in court:

> Members of any chartered organization shall be regularly enrolled high school students from one high school student body. Graduates or students who have dropped from school shall not be permitted to retain membership. Public school students who were bona fide members of an interschool club prior to October 27, 1949, may retain membership in any club that qualifies for a charter.

The Supreme Court of Oregon ruled in favor of the school board by saying that pupils " . . . have no constitutional right to be members of clubs . . . which the school board may have substantial reason for believing to be inimical to the discipline and effective operation of the schools."[10]

---

[10] Burkitt v. School Dist. No. 1, Multnomah County, 195 Ore 471, 246 P(2d) 566 (1952).

In an early case, the Supreme Court of Iowa concluded that a school board acted within its authority when a group of pupils was prohibited from engaging in football games on and away from school premises.[11]

The board of directors of the Independent School District of Marion established the following rule regarding the playing of football:

> Resolved, that the board of directors disfavor football on account of injuries to life and limb. The board will lend all assistance, morally and financially, in support of baseball, the gymnasium, or track work, but for the above reasons will not permit football or practice under the auspices of the High School or on the school grounds.

This regulation was violated by a group of pupils of Marion High School who played, on a Saturday afternoon, another high school team at the local fair grounds. Advertisements were posted which represented the game as one between Marion High School and West Branch High School.

One of the boys, suspended from school for his participation in this game, brought suit for a writ of mandamus to compel the defendants to admit him to the privileges of the high school.

In the opinion of the court, Chief Justice McClain stressed the position generally taken by the courts that the management of the schools should be left to the discretion of the board of education and not the courts. The court, therefore, upheld the right of the school district to control out-of-class activities away from the school premises if the pupils purported to represent the school:

> They [the directors] have no concern, it is true, with the individual conduct of the pupils wholly outside of the school room and the school grounds and while they are presumed to be under the control of their parents, or after they are beyond the age of parental control, to be governed by the rules which regulate the conduct of all members of the body politic; but the conduct of pupils

---

[11] Kinzer v. Directors of Independ. Sch. Dist. of Marion, 129 Iowa 441, 105 NW 686 (1906).

which directly relates to and affects the management of the school and its efficiency is within the proper regulation of the school authorities. . . . We have no doubt as to the power of the defendant board, in the exercise of its reasonable discretion as to the management of the high school, to determine that it was detrimental to the best interests of the school that pupils should be encouraged by their school associates to engage in games of football with teams of other high schools, and we think that their proper power, with reference to encouragement or discouragement of the playing of football by pupils of the school, was not limited to the high school grounds, but extended to participation by the pupils in games as members of a team purporting to represent in any way the high school under control of defendant board; and we therefore reach the conclusion that . . . such rule was not unreasonable nor in excess of the powers of the board.

In Tennessee the state legislature passed a statute which prohibited bands and orchestras of public institutions, supported by state revenues, from competing with professional musicians. The statute read as follows:

The intent and purpose of this Act, as an expression of the public policy of this State, is to avoid and prevent such bands or orchestras from in any and every possible way competing with and making unnecessary· the employment of civilian musicians. [12]

The main objective behind this statute was the control of school bands, for no other state institutions had bands or orchestras.

The Memphis Federation of Musicians, Local No. 71, sought to enforce this law. Suit was then brought to enjoin the expenditure of union funds to enforce the provisions of this act. The Supreme Court of Tennessee, upon hearing the appeal, concluded that the law was unenforceable because its primary objective was not the control of pupils participating

---

[12] Gentry v. Memphis Federation of Musicians, 177 Tenn 566, 151 SW(2d) 1001 (1941).

in school activities by the protection and profit of another group of residents of the state: professional musicians. In the opinion of the court, Chief Justice Green pointed out that it was within the power of the state to pass laws for the government of the schools, but that all such laws must have a direct relationship to the welfare of the public school system.

It is within the power of the state to prohibit students in any of its schools from joining a band, or if school bands are countenanced, the State might restrict the appearances or performances of these bands to limited occasions. These things might be done as a matter of discipline to prevent the time and interest of students being too greatly diverted from their school work proper.

. . . The act before us, however, disavows any purpose to promote discipline in the State's institutions or otherwise benefit such institutions.

The act . . . is not an effort to exercise the State's power in the interests of its institutions nor in the interests of the beneficiaries of those institutions.

. . . .

The act does not seek to regulate the activities of students as such, but attempts to regulate the activities of citizens, who happen to be students, in their relations with other citizens.

. . . .

These students are entitled to the benefits of the State's institutions under general laws. We think their extracurricular activities can not be penalized as here attempted for the declared purpose and the sole purpose of profit to another group of citizens.

It is an established legal principle that the state has the authority, either by specific statutory provisions or by delegating powers to school boards, to govern the extracurricular program of the public schools by the passage of rules and regulations that are needed to achieve the purposes and objectives of the schools, so long as such rules and regulations are not arbitrary, unreasonable, and discriminatory. Therefore, the majority of the cases dealing with rules and regulations pertaining to extracurricular activities are brought before the courts on the grounds that the school board exceeded its constitutional limits for the government of the schools or passed resolutions which were arbitrary, unreasonable, or discriminatory. In this area of litigation most of the cases heard by the courts deal with the authority of school boards to prohibit secret society members and married pupils from participating in extracurricular activities.

§ 3.3   Authority of school officials to regulate extracurricular participation of secret society members

The first case challenging the authority of a school board to prohibit members of a high school fraternity from participating in extracurricular activities occurred in the state of Washington.[13]

Gamma Eta Kappa fraternity was first organized in Seattle in 1900. Immediately a request was made by this society to use the name of Seattle High School in connection with the fraternity. The school authorities conducted an investigation to determine the probable effect of a fraternity associated with the high school. After receiving reports from prominent educators, all of whom condemned the influence of high school fraternities as deleterious, the school board, on May 7, 1901, denied the Gamma Eta Kappa fraternity the privilege of associating with Seattle High School. Thereafter it was contrary to school rules for pupils to become members of the fraternity. Nevertheless, George Wayland and some other pupils did become members.

On May 5, 1905, the board of education passed a resolution which gave full school privileges to all fraternity members and pledges who would promise not to join any other secret society or solicit additional membership for their organization or in any way support a secret society. Those fraternity members who failed to make this promise were restricted to classwork and prohoibited from participating in school organizations such as debating clubs, athletic teams, school bands, glee clubs, orchestras, and cadet corps.

---

[13] Wayland v. Board of School Directors of Dist. No. 1 of Seattle, 43 Wash 441, 86 Pac 642 (1906).

Suit was brought in the superior court of King County by Russel Wayland in behalf of his eighteen-year-old son, George, and the members of Gamma Eta Kappa fraternity. The contention was that the fraternity members, all of school age, were unjustly prohibited from belonging to extra-curricular groups. According to Wayland the regulation was in excess of lawful authority, for there was nothing objectionable in a fraternity which met outside of school and under parental control. The plaintiff sought to restrain the board of education from enforcing the rule which he declared deprived Greek letter fraternities of the privileges of high school other than attending classes. When the trial court refused the injunctive relief sought by the plaintiff, an appeal was taken to the Supreme Court of Washington.

The supreme court had to determine whether the board of education had the authority to adopt the contested regulation. The court said that the board of education did not prohibit fraternity membership or school attendance. They only sought to prevent the fraternity members from dictating the terms on which they would enjoy certain privileges which were incidental to the regular school curriculum. The court held that the board of education did not invade the authority of the home by restricting fraternity members, for it was proved that fraternities had a marked influence on the school by tending to destroy good order and discipline. In a situation such as the one which existed here the board of education had the discretionary authority, if not the duty, to take reasonable action to prevent such influences. In this regard the court said: "These powers have been properly and legally conferred upon the board, and unless it arbitrarily exceeds its authority, which it has not done here, the court cannot interfere with its actions."

Several years later, the Supreme Court of Illinois upheld a resolution passed by the Chicago Board of Education which prohibited students who were secret society members from representing the public schools in literary or athletic contests. [14]

---

[14] Wilson v. Board of Ed. of Chicago, 233 Ill 464, 84 NE 697 (1908).

A bill was filed in behalf of four pupils, all members of Phi Sigma fraternity, to enjoin the board of education from enforcing this rule. The plaintiffs charged that the adoption of the rule was an exercise of arbitrary power by the board of education and was a violation of the natural rights of the fraternity members and an unlawful discrimination against them. After failure to receive favorable judgments in both the superior and appellate courts, the case went to the supreme court on a writ of error to the appellate court.

The supreme court ruled that the board of education had a duty to make rules and regulations to insure a " . . . proper and uniform system of discipline in the . . . schools." The rule only deprived the fraternity members of the privilege of representing the public schools in literary and athletic contests. They were not denied membership in extracurricular activities, nor were they prohibited from receiving the same benefits from these activities that pupils not members of secret societies received. Since the fraternity members were only prohibited from representing the schools as members of extracurricular groups in public contests, the court ruled that this regulation was neither a denial of natural rights nor unlawfully discriminatory.

In affirming the judgment of the appellate court, the supreme court said in part:

> Pupils attending the schools may decide for themselves whether they prefer membership in the secret societies, with the disqualification from representing their schools in literary or athletic contests or other public capacities, or whether they prefer these latter privileges to membership in said societies. It is for the board of education, within the reasonable exercise of power and discretion, to say what is best for the successful management and conduct of the schools . . . .

Shortly thereafter the Supreme Court of Illinois again handed down an identical ruling in a per curiam decision in another case dealing with the same regulation and the same question of law. [15]

---

[15] Favorite v. Board of Ed. of Chicago, 235 Ill 314, 85 NE 402 (1908).

The Supreme Court of Missouri, in one of the few decisions not upholding the authority of school boards, ruled that pupils who were secret society members could not be prohibited from participating in extracurricular activities. [16]

The board of education of St. Louis adopted a rule prohibiting secret society members from participating in extracurricular activities and graduation exercises. The regulation was recommened by the superintendent of schools because of the undesirable influences resulting from society activities. The purpose of the action was to enjoin the board of education from enforcing the rule declaring pupils who were secret society members ineligible for membership in any organization supported by the school.

Suit was brought against the school district in the St. Louis Circuit Court. Upon receiving an adverse judgment the plaintiff appealed to the supreme court. After reviewing the record the court said:

> There is nothing shown as to the conduct of the pupils alleged to be within the purview of the rule to support the conclusion that their membership in the societies designated has proved detrimental to the operation and control of the school. In the absence of such evidence, the reason for the rule, so far as this case is concerned, ceases to exist.

In relation to the school board's discretionary power the Supreme Court of Missouri took a view different from that expressed by the Supreme Court of Washington in *Wayland v. Board of School Directors of Seattle, supra:*

> It will suffice . . . to say that it [discretionary power] should extend no further than may be found reasonably necessary to promote the intelligent conduct and control of the school. . . .Any other interpretation would remove all limit to the exercise of discretionary power, leaving it to the judgment, whim, or caprice of each succeeding board [of education]. We have not reached that point in the interpretation of a delegated power where, with a proper regard for the rights of citizens and the rules of

---

[16] Wright v. Board of Ed. of St. Louis, 295 Mo 466, 246 SW 43 (1922).

construction, we feel authorized in holding . . . that the board's power is to be limited only by its discretion free from all determination by the courts.

Justices Blair and Elder dissented because in their opinion a regulation as the board of education had imposed was necessary to improve discipline within the school, since there was evidence that secret society members had poorer grades and were greater discipline problems than other pupils. Their contention that this regulation was reasonable and was within the discretionary power of the board of education to enact is expressed in the dissenting opinion written by Justice Blair:

> The board [of education] clearly has [the] power to make all reasonable rules to promote efficiency, order, and discipline in the schools and to prevent the contrary. If it be conceded that the conduct and activities of students, whether during or after school hours, tend to destroy such efficiency, order, and discipline in the schools themselves, rules denouncing such conduct and providing penalties therefor are necessarily reasonable. In determining whether the conduct of any student or set of students has such effect, the courts should yield largely to the discretion and judgment of the board and require the unreasonableness of the rule to be shown by those attacking it, rather than to require the board to establish the reasonableness of the rule in the first instance, as the majority opinion seems to require.

In a North Carolina case the state supreme court ruled that a school board did not violate the rights of pupils by refusing to permit high school fraternity members to participate in extracurricular activities. [17]

The Durham City Board of Education made the signing of the following pledge a prerequisite to participation in all extracurricular activities:

> Here appears a declaration that the signer is not a member or "pledge" of any fraternity or society not approved by the school board; that he will not join any such society

---

[17] Coggin v. Board of Ed. of Durham, 223 NC 763, 28 SE(2d) 527 (1944).

or attend the meetings of same or any function sponsored by it; and that he will not contribute funds to or participate in any of the activities of any such organization.

Those pupils who failed to sign the pledge were barred from the following activities:

1. Holding any office of Student Body, Homeroom Class, or Club
2. Taking part in all intra-mural and interscholastic activities or contests, both Athletic and Literary
3. Representing the school or class or any organization in any capacity
4. Serving as Editors or Managers of school publications, or writing articles therefor
5. Taking part in the Senior play or other dramatic activities
6. Participating in Assembly or Homeroom program
7. Serving as Cafeteria or Library helper
8. Attending High School dances or socials
9. Serving as Monitors in any capacity
10. Becoming a member of any school-sponsored club, society or organization
11. Representing the school in Student Government activities

John Rod Coggin, Jr., a member of Phi Kappa Delta fraternity, sued the board of education because, as he said, it deprived him of the right to become a member of the football team and other extracurricular organizations. He contended that unless he signed the pledge he was denied privileges and advantages guaranteed by the public school laws of the state of North Carolina. When the superior court of Durham County issued a temporary restraining order, the defendant school board demurred by contending that the complaint did not state facts sufficient to constitute a cause of action. After the court entered judgment sustaining the demurrer and dismissing the action, the plaintiff appealed to the Supreme Court of North Carolina.

The supreme cout in declaring that each pupil of the state had a right to attend the public school emphasized the need for reasonable rules and regulations for governing the schools:

> The State provides free educational facilities for the children of the state, and each child has the right to attend the schools of his district. But this is not an absolute right. Schools to be effective and fulfill the purposes for which they are intended must be operated in an orderly manner. Machinery to that end must be provided. Reasonable rules and regulations must be adopted. The right to attend school and claim the benefits afforded by the public school system is the right to attend subject to all rules and regulations prescribed for the government thereof. This is all the plaintiff may claim.

The court held that the school board did not deny Coggin any instruction in the required curriculum of the school. Participation in extracurricular activities was not denied him; it was only made optional.

> The rule makes no attempt to deny plaintiff any instruction afforded by class work or by the required curriculum of the school. Nor is he denied the right to participate in extra-curricular activites. It is merely made optional with him to determine whether, against the known wishes of the school authorities, he prefers to continue his membership in a secret society and thereby forfeit participation in the privileges afforded by the extra-curricular activities of the schools, which, by compliance with the rule, would be available to him. He has now arrived at one of the cross roads of life. He must decide which course he will take, and the choice is his.

Since the court concluded that the board of education acted in good faith and within its power the plaintiff was not, contrary to his contention, denied any right guaranteed to him by the public school laws of North Carolina.

In a similar case, the court of civil appeals of Texas upheld the right of a school board to limit the activities of secret society members to classroom work. [18]

---

[18] Wilson v. Abilene Independ. Sch. Dist., 190 SW(2d) 406 (Texas, 1945).

The board of trustees of the Abilene Independent School District passed a resolution requiring junior and senior high school pupils to sign a pledge stating that they were not secret society members or pledges. The signing of this pledge was a prerequisite to the participation in extracurricular activities, the holding of school offices, and the receiving of honors. The pledge, to be honored during vacation periods, was to be effective until graduation. A pupil was prohibited from participating in the following activities if either he or his parents refused to sign the pledge:

1. Holding class or club offices
2. Taking part in inter- and intra-school contests, both athletic and literary
3. Representing the school, a class, or any organization in any capacity
4. Writing articles for the school paper
5. Taking part in plays
6. Graduating with honor
7. Participating in assembly programs
8. Serving as office helper, library assistant, or hall patrol
9. Receiving medals or scholarships

The parents of several minor children brought suit in the district court of Taylor County. Seeking a permanent and perpetual injunction against the school board, the plaintiffs prayed for a temporary injunction to prevent the defendants from enforcing the order, pending final determination of the suit. When the court refused the application for injunction the plaintiffs appealed to the court of civil appeals of Texas.

The plaintiffs contended that the rule was beyond the statutory or implied authority of the board of education and was unreasonable, arbitrary, discriminatory, and violative of parental authority. The questions for the court to answer were whether the board of education had the power to make and enforce the regulation and, if such power existed, whether the passing of the resolution in question was a reasonable action.

In upholding the right of the school board to make such a rule the court said:

> . . . [S] chool boards are given a wide discretion in such matters. They may make all such rules and regulations as in their judgment are necessary to maintain an "efficient" system of schools, subject to limitation that there be no abuse of discretion, and that such regulation be not arbitrary, unreasonable or in violation of the law.

The court concluded that the board of education, by conducting a survey and proceeding very cautiously, illustrated a need for the regulation, and did not abuse its discretion by adopting such a regulation except in extending it to include vacation periods. This portion of the regulation, which the court regarded as practically unenforceable, was declared an invasion of parental authority.

After years of secret society trouble and difficulty in regulating fraternity members, the board of education of Little Rock, Arkansas, passed a rule to prohibit members from participating in extracurricular activities and receiving honors. Members of secret societies were declared ineligible for the following offices, honors, and activities:

1. Homeroom positions, political and social
2. Inter-School Sports: football, basketball, track, and any other contests which are scheduled after school
3. Band, Choral Groups, and Glee Club
4. Committee approintments from the Student Council, Girls' Council, and Athletic Council
5. Any office in the Student Body Association
6. Scholastic Honors: Honor Roll, National Honor Society, etc.
7. Class Honors: Tiger Editorial Staff, Banquet Toastmaster, etc.
8. Miscellaneous: The policy includes all honors given by the faculty or by the student body

Ben Isgrig brought suit for a restraining order against the Little Rock School District to prevent enforcement of the regulation. When the trial court issued a decree dismissing the complaint, the plaintiff appealed to the Supreme Court of

Arkansas.[19] Since the board of education had the power under existing statutes and discretionary authority to regulate fraternities and sororities, the court said that the school directors could " . . . impose reasonable restrictions in those instances where experience, observation, and a knowledge of the, . . . [situation] being dealt with suggest[ed] this course."

For reasons similar to those given by the Little Rock School District, the board of education of Wichita, Kansas, passed the following resolution:

> Be it Therefore Resolved that the school administrators be instructed to deny all members, active or inactive, alumni or pledges, or in any degree affiliated with the Tally Ho, Tally Hostess Sub-Debs or other similar organizations, participation in any extracurricular school activities.

Suit was brought in the Sedgwick District Court by several girls who were members of the organizations mentioned in the resolution. The court denied relief and the plaintiffs appealed to the Supreme Court of Kansas.[20] The appeal did not reach the supreme court until June 6, 1953, and since the girls involved were graduated on June 1, 1953, the case was moot. In spite of the appellees' contention that the question involved was of public interest and should be decided, the court dismissed the appeal.

The most recent case dealing with the right of a school board to prohibit students who belong to social clubs from participating in extracurricular activities occurred in Ohio.[21]

Pupils who were members of secret societies were forbidden the opportunity to participate in any athletic, literary, military, musical, dramatic, science, or scholastic activity outside of the regular school curriculum.

The parents of two girls sought an injunction against the board of education of the city of Columbus. The plaintiffs said that their daughters belonged to a group which was iden-

---

[19] Isgrig v. Srygley, 210 Ark 580, 197 SW(2d) 39 (1946).
[20] Andeel v. Woods, 174 Kan 556, 258 P(2d) 285 (1953).
[21] Holroyd v. Eibling, 188 NE(2d) 208 (CP, Ohio, 1961), 188 NE(2d) 797 (Ohio, 1962).

tified with an adult service organization. This group, according to the plaintiffs, was not a sorority, did not have a secret initiation or ritual, and existed for the purpose of encouraging school and community participation. The plaintiffs contended that enforcement of this rule would deny parents the right to select their childrens' associates.

Although there is no statutory provision in Ohio expressly granting to the school board the power to make such a rule, the court ruled that the board of education acted within its discretionary authority. The regulation, which was neither unreasonable nor arbitrary, did not deprive pupils of any rights. In upholding the ruling of a lower court, the court of appeals of Ohio said that it had no authority in a discretionary matter of this nature.

With only one exception, the Supreme Court of Missouri in *Wright* v. *Board of Education of St. Louis, supra,* the courts have rendered decisions favorable to boards of education when their authority to prohibit secret society members from participating in extracurricular activities was challenged.

§ 3.4 Authority of school officials to regulate extra-curricular participation of married students

Failing in their attempt to exclude married students from attending public schools, some boards of education have used other restrictive measures to discourage high school marriages,[22] in spite of evidence which indicates that restrictive policies do not successfully prevent or discourage teenage marriages.[23] In a survey conducted in North Carolina, it was discovered that a majority of the schools sampled restricted partially or entirely the participation of married students in extracurricular activities.[24]

In all the cases to reach the higher courts, school boards were upheld in their action prohibiting married students from

---

[22] Anne Flowers and Edward C. Bolmeier, Law and Pupil Control, Cincinnati, Ohio: The W. H. Anderson Company, 1964, p. 60.

[23] Lee G. Burchinal, "Do Restrictive Policies Curb Teen Marriages?" Overview, I (March, 1960), pp. 72-73.

[24] Judson Landis, "Attitudes and Policies Concerning Marriages Among High School Students," Marriage and Family Living, XVIII (May, 1956), pp. 128-36.

participating in extracurricular activities, but the question has been decided in too few cases to say definitely that a legal precedent has been established.

It is questionable whether the school board has the legal authority to restrict married students to classroom work on the sole basis of their marital status. "If it could be proved that marriage in itself is detrimental to the student involved or to the morale of the school in all instances, a board [of education] regulation. . . . designed to curb marriages would have some justification."[25] In the absence of evidence that the married students disrupt the good order and discipline of the school, a board of education, by passing a resolution prohibiting these students from participating in extracurricular activities, might well be acting unreasonably, arbitrarily, and in a discriminatory manner.[26]

The opinion that legal marriage, a higly respected social institution which is sanctioned by the law, should present no problem to the public schools was expressed by the attorney general of Florida:[27]

> As marriage is a domestic relation sanctioned by religion and favored by the law, the effect of a married pupil attending the public schools would ordinarily appear to be good, rather than bad, and a married person could reasonably be expected to exercise a refining influence on the other pupils of the school. It is commendable in married persons of school age to further their education and thereby be better fitted for life's work and its duties.

A similar view toward the state of matrimony was presented in *McLeod* v. *Mississippi*.[28] The question then arises as to the legality and propriety of penalizing a student for marrying, since marriage is recognized by the state as being

---

[25] E. C. Bolmeier, "Legality and Propriety of School Board Regulations Designed to Govern High School Marriages," Proceedings of the Second School Law Conference, Appalachian State Teachers College (Boone, North Carolina: Appalachian State Teachers College, 1963), p. 18

[26] Kentucky Attorney General Opinions 1960-1964, OAG 62-996, pp. 2-931-33.

[27] Biennial Report of the Attorney General of Florida, 1951-52, 052-328, pp. 386-89.

[28] McLeod v. Mississippi, 154 Miss 468, 122 So 737 (1929).

consistent with public policy. In an opinion given in 1962, the attorney general of Ohio reasoned that school boards were without authority to restrict extracurricular participation of married students: [29]

> In developing a program of education which meets the minimum standards adopted by the state board of education for the education of Ohio youths, boards of education have uniformly included a multitude of extracurricular activities. Such activities have become an integral part of contemporary education and to deprive a student from participating in such activities for the dubious purpose of punishing marriage would amount to an abuse of discretion. For this reason . . . I am of the opinion that a board of education may not lawfully adopt a regulation prohibiting married students from participation in extra-curricular activities fostered and promoted by the school as part of the regular school program; and may not adopt a regulation automatically prohibiting the attendance of married pregnant students at such activities, except that a board of education may adopt a rule which would, for the physical safety of the student, require that at an advanced stage of pregnancy a pregnant student not attend such activities.

The status of marriage in some states gives minors more privileges than they enjoy before marrying. A few states bestow majority rights on married minors by statutory provisions: "The period of minority extends to the age of twenty-one years, but all minors attain their majority by marriage, and females, after reaching the age of eighteen years, may make valid contracts for marriage the same as adults." [30] Several other states which grant majority rights to married minors are Florida, [31] Kansas, [32] and Utah. [33]

---

[29] Opinions of the Attorney General of Ohio, 1962, No. 2998, (mimeographed form).
[30] Iowa Code Annotated, Vol. 39, Section 599.1.
[31] Florida Statutes Annotated, Vol. 21A, Section 743.01.
[32] General Statutes of Kansas Annotated, 1949, Chapter 38, Article 1, Section 38-101.
[33] Utah Code Annotated, Vol. 2, Section 15-2-1.

The granting of majority rights to married high school students raises the question as to whether these persons are, by virtue of their new status, eligible to attend the public schools in which the upper limit for attendance is twenty-one years of age. The courts have never decided this question in relation to public school attendance laws. However, in a Florida case the court ruled that a married minor woman who had attained her majority by statute was illegally employed by a vendor of alcoholic beverages under a statute which prohibited persons under twenty-one years of age from engaging in such employment.[34]

A practical problem for administrators who do restrict the activities of married pupils is that of the status of a student who is divorced or whose marriage has been annuled. Again, a question of law is here involved which has never been decided in the courts. The only clue as to how a court might rule must of necessity stem from the meaning of the terms "divorce" and "annulment."

Divorce is the legal separation of husband and wife, for cause, by the judgment of a court which either totally dissolves the marriage relation, or suspends its effects so far as concerns the cohabitation of the parties.[35] An annulment is an act making void retrospectively as well as prospectively.[36]

Action for a divorce is distinguished from one for annulment, in that "divorce action" is predicated on valid marriage and decree terminates relationship from date thereof, while "annulment" destroys existence of void or voidable marriage and everything appertaining thereto from the beginning.[37]

From this distinction it can be concluded that the two decrees, divorce and annulment, are not the same and that the legal status of the parties under each of these decrees will differ. The attorney general of Iowa in one of his opinions differentiated between the two decrees:[38]

34 Hunter v. Bullington, 74 S(2d) 673 (Fla, 1954).
35 Henry C. Black (Ed.), Black's Law Dictionary, St. Paul, Minn.: West Publishing Co., 1951, p. 566.
36 Ibid., p. 177.
37 Wigder v. Wigder, 14 NJ 880, 188 Atl 235 (1936).
38 Report of the Attorney General (Iowa), 1923-24, pp. 330-31.

. . . [I] t is my opinion that in the case of divorce, the decree for divorce has no retroactive effect per se, that is, it does not of itself restore the status quo of the parties before marriage. The legal operation and effect of a decree of annulment is to render the marriage contract nullity, and consequently the status of the parties is restored the same as though the marriage had never been consummated.

The foregoing questions have to remain unanswered for want of court cases establishing legal precedent. Until these issues are settled by the courts, the wise administrator should be aware of the existing problems and familiar with the rulings handed down in the cases which do exist.

Cases dealing with the authority of school officials to prohibit married students from participating in extracurricular activities, while few in number, have increased in recent years. The first of the five recorded cases occurred in Texas in 1959.[39]

Jerry Kissick, Jr., a student at Garland Public Schools, was a letterman on his 1958 high school football team and was looking forward to an athletic scholarship for college. In March, 1959, he married and was thereafter prohibited from participating in athletic activities. Although participation in football was sufficient to earn credit for the required physical education course, Kissick was not permitted to play football during the 1959 season.

Upon receiving an adverse decision in seeking an injunction in the circuit court of Dallas County, Kissick appealed to the court of civil appeals of Texas. He contended that the school board resolution was void because it was, among other things, arbitrary, capricious, discriminatory, and unreasonable and violative of public policy because it penalized marriage.

After considering the findings of a parent-teacher association study group and the testimony of a professional psychologist, who was also a member of the school board, the court concluded that the board of education resolution prohibiting married students from participating in extracurricular activities was neither arbitrary nor unreasonable, for it had a

---

[39] Kissick v. Garland Independ. Sch. Dist., 330 SW(2d) 708 (Tex, 1959).

direct relationship to the objectives of the school board: the discouragement of teenage marriages. In the opinion of the court, the findings of the PTA group and the professional psychologist clearly indicated a need for such a resolution. The court also pointed out that the resolution was consistent with state limitations and regulations regarding youthful marriages. Thus, the appeal was overruled and the ruling of the lower court affirmed.

A similar case came before the Michigan courts in 1960.[40] Ronald Cochrane and David Shively, students in the Messick Consolidated School District, participated in sports during their junior year in high school and hoped to do likewise as seniors. Both boys married during the summer of 1958, and when they returned to school they were subject to the following rule which became effective on August 28, 1958: "Married students attending school shall not be eligible to participate in any co-curricular activities: . . . competitive sports, band, glee club, class and club offices, cheer leading, physical education, [and] class plays. . . ." One of the reasons given by the board of education for enacting the rule was the possibility of bad influence of the married pupils on the unmarried students of the school. Also, if teenage marriages were not condemned by the board of education other pupils might regard marriage as an acceptable action and mimic their friends who were married. The extra time required by the additional responsibilities of marriage was also given as a reason for restricting married pupils to classroom work.

The two athletes and their fathers brought suit in the circuit court of Wexford County for a writ of mandamus to compel the board of education to admit married students to extracurricular activities. In court it was indicated that the resolution was passed to prevent the possible bad influence of married pupils on those who were not married, but the superintendent testified that the boys in question were good students and were not disciplinary problems.

From an adverse decision in the circuit court, the plaintiffs and the attorney general, who intervened, appealed to the

[40] Cochrane v. Board of Ed. of the Messick Consol. Sch. Dist., 360 Mich 390, 103 NW(2d) 569 (1960).

Supreme Court of Michigan. The attorney general requested that the supreme court provide an authoritative determination of the issues involved in this case because they were important public questions.

In the opinion written by Justice Kelly, in which Justices Carr, Smith, and Edwards concurred, it was stated:

The reasons advanced by the board, endeavoring to justify its action, are not persuasive or convincing. . . . .

. . . .

Denying a married student the right to education, whether a partial denial such as denying the right to participate in extracurricular activities, or a complete denial such as expulsion or suspension, was not a responsible exercise of authority by a school board or school officials.

There was no reason for denying plaintiffs the right to participate in extra-curricular activities, other than the fact that they had married. The action of the school board was arbitrary and unreasonable.

The order of the lower court is set aside and the resolution of the Messick consolidated school district excluding married students from co-curricular activities is declared null and void.

However, Justice Kavanagh, in an opinion in which Justices Dethmers and Black concurred, expressed a differing view:

No clear abuse has been shown when all facts and circumstances are considered, such as size and type of community, size of school, number of students dropping out of school attributed to marriage, and the resulting effect on other students. It was within the power of the defendant school board to adopt the rule in question.

Justice Souris concurred in the decision reached by Justice Kavanagh but for different reasons. He said: "I concur in the result reached by Justice Kavanagh, but only on the ground that the question presented is moot."

Since this was a moot case by the time it reached the supreme court, the opinion was only advisory and the ruling by the circuit court upholding the action of the school board had to stand.

The school board of Hamilton, Ohio, established a "Code of Ethics" in which was incorporated a clause prohibiting married pupils from joining extracurricular organizations of the school. The regulation read as follows: " . . . [M] arried students in the Hamilton schools will not be permitted to participate in extracurricular activities, effective as of the opening of the 1962-63 school year."

The school authorities felt that this regulation was necessary to discourage early marriages which were a contributory factor to the dropout problems in the schools. The board of education also thought that by prohibiting the star athletes who were married from participating in competitive sports, their "hero" image would not be so influential on their peers and the desire on the part of other teenagers to imitate their idols would be weakened. In addition to these reasons it was stressed that the extra time needed for carrying out the responsibilities of married life did not afford students the extra time needed for extracurricular activities.

A suit was filed in the court of common pleas of Ohio, Butler County, by a senior at Taft High School, Hamilton, Ohio, who prayed for a writ of mandamus against the board of education and the superintendent of schools to permit him, a married student, to engage in basketball.[41] The relator contended that the rule was arbitrary, unreasonable, and discriminatory and was a violation of public policy since it penalized marriage.

In regard to the relator's first charge the court said:

> In our opinion, it cannot be successfully claimed that the Respondent Board was unreasonable or arbitrary or abused its discretion, in concluding as it has, that marriage by the high school student causes the student to quit or drop out of school; nor in concluding that the married student engaging in extra-curricular activities sets a pattern which his or her fellow students follow; nor in concluding that participation by such a student in extra-curricular

---

[41] State ex rel. Baker v. Stevenson, 27 OhioOp(2d) 223, 189 NE(2d) 181 (1962).

activities might interfere with and seriously affect that student's responsibilities as a husband and father; nor in concluding that the marriage has a better chance of lasting where interests of the husband or wife outside of and not connected with the home or marriage as such, are kept to a minimum.

The court also disagreed with the relator's secondcharge that the institution of matrimony was penalized by the school board's regulation: "Any policy which is directed toward making juvenile marriages unpopular and to be avoided should have the general public's wholehearted approval and support."

In a Utah case, the board of education was upheld in its right to prohibit married students from participating in extracurricular activities. [42] The board of education desired to discourage early marriages because they were a contributing factor to the dropout problem. It was also the consensus of the board of education that, for those students already married, the additional time required by extracurricular activities could more effectively be given to the responsibilities of marriage.

James Harold Starkey, a senior, married during the 1962-63 Christmas vacation, and was thereafter barred from participating in the Boys' Association, the usher squad, and the wrestling team. Starkey, who also wanted to play baseball, brought suit in the district court of Davis County. After receiving an adverse judgment, he appealed the case to the Supreme Court of Utah. He said that the regulation was contrary to the Utah constitution, which provides for a "uniform system of public schools, which shall be open to all children of the State. . . ." It was his contention that extracurricular activities, as well as academic subjects, are part of the total public school program.

In the opinion of the court, extracurricular activities were those endeavors which carried no credit and were supplementary to the regular academic curriculum, but which were carried out under the discretionary powers granted to the

---

[42] Starkey v. Board of Ed. of Davis County Sch. Dist., 14 Utah (2d) 227, 381 P(2d) 718 (1963).

board of education. The court felt that the extent to which the extracurricular activities were made available to the students was up to the board of education: "Their authority extends to making reasonable rules and regulations calculated to serve the purpose of education. This, of course, includes the prescribing of qualifications for students to participate." So long as the standards for eligibility are based on uniform classifications which are related to the objectives of the school they " . . . cannot be said to be capricious, arbitrary, or unjustly discriminatory."

In relation to the providing of equal privileges under a uniform system of public education the court had the following to say:

> We have no disagreement with the proposition advocated that all students attending school should be accorded equal privileges and advantages. But the participation in extracurricular activities must necessarily be subject to regulation as to eligibility. Engaging in them is a privilege which may be claimed only to accordance with the standards set up for participation. It is conceded, as plaintiff insists, that he has a constitutional right to get married. But he has no "right" to compel the Board of Education to exercise its discretion to his personal advantage so he can participate in the named activities.

In a 1967 case, the Supreme Court of Iowa upheld a board of education regulation prohibiting married students from participating in extracurricular activities. [42a]

By the time this case was appealed to the Supreme Court of Iowa, it was moot, but the court decided to hear it for the following reason: "when the issue presented is of substantial public interest there exists a permissible exception to the general rule that a case which has become moot or presents only an academic question will be dismissed on appeal."

In upholding the rule prohibiting married students from participating in extracurricular activities, the court said:

> We do not consider the rule here in question to be violative of public policy in that it penalizes persons because

---

[42a] Board of Directors of the Independent School District of Waterloo v. Green, 147 NE(2d) 854 (Iowa, 1967).

of marriage. The law looks with favor upon this most vital social institution. However, that policy is basically referrable to those of lawful age who enter into the marital relationship. As to underage marriages the legislative policy is said to be otherwise.

Although they did not write a dissenting opinion, three of the justices reviewing this case dissented. There appears to be judicial disagreement as to the legality of rules and regulations restricting married pupils to classroom activities solely on the basis of their marital status.

The courts have, without exception, upheld the right of boards of education to make rules and regulations prohibiting married students from participating in extracurricular activities, so long as the restrictions were oriented toward the objectives of the school system and were not unreasonable, arbitrary, or discriminatory. However, the number of cases in which this question has been decided is too few, and the question too controversial, to say that a definite legal principle has been established. The advisory opinion given by the Supreme Court of Michigan in *Cochrane* v. *Board of Education, supra,* is of interest because of the possible future influence it might have in the courts. Four of the justices concluded that " . . . [d] enying a married student . . . the right to participate in extracurricular activities . . . was not a responsible exercise of authority by a school board or school officials."

§ 3.5   Summary

Although most state constituions provide for a uniform system of public schools, it is not mandatory for every school to offer identical programs or even provide identical educational opportunities for each of its pupils. The welfare of the state, the primary purpose of public education, requires that limits be placed on the freedom of individual pupils by imposing such rules and regulations as are required for the efficient government of the school. In the course of governing a school it is necessary to enforce regulations which control the activities of pupils. School boards have the authority to make rules and regulations which, in the interest of promoting the objectives of the school, prohibit certain pupils from participating in the total school program.

There is, however, a point beyond which school officials cannot go without violating individual rights guaranteed by the United States Constitution. This point is determined by the courts on the basis of the reasonableness of the regulation involved in each case. Rules and regulations pertaining to extracurricular activities which are most frequently challenged as being arbitrary, unreasonable, and discriminatory are those restricting secret society members and married students to class room activities.

The courts in Washington,[43] North Carolina,[44] Texas,[45] Arkansas,[46] Kansas,[47] and Ohio,[48] have upheld the right of a school board to restrict secret society members to classroom activities. A resolution passed by the Chicago Board of Education which prohibited secret society members from representing the public schools in literary and athletic contests was upheld by the Supreme Court of Illinois.[49]

The only court to render a decision adverse to the school board was the Supreme Court of Missouri.[50] The majority of the court reasoned that there was nothing shown to prove that the conduct of secret society members was detrimental to the discipline and control of the school. The court therefore concluded that a regulation prohibiting secret society members from participating in extracurricular activities was unnecessary and beyond the discretionary power of the board of education to enforce.

In an effort to discourage high school marriages, some school boards have passed resolutions barring married students from extracurricular activities. Although it is question-

---

[43] Wayland v. Board of School Directors of Dist. No. 1 of Seattle, 43 Wash 441, 86 Pac 642 (1906).

[44] Coggin v. Board of Ed. of Durhan, 223 NC 763, 28 SE(2d) 527 (1944).

[45] Wilson v. Abilene Independ. Sch. Dist., 190 SW(2d) 406 (Tex, 1945).

[46] Isgrig v. Srygley, 210 Ark 580, 197 SW(2d) 39 (1946).

[47] Andeel v. Woods, 174 Kan 556, 258 P(2d) 285 (1953).

[48] Holroyd v. Eibling, 188 NE(2d) 208 (CP, Ohio, 1961), 188 NE(2d) 797 (Ohio, 1962).

[49] Wilson v. Board of Ed. of Chicago, 233 Ill 464, 84 NE 697 (1908); Favorite v. Board of Ed. of Chicago, 235 Ill 314, 85 NE 402 (1908).

[50] Wright v. Board of Ed. of St. Louis, 295 Mo 466, 246 SW 43 (1922).

able whether a school board can legally restrict married
students to classroom work, the courts, in the few cases involving this question, have always ruled in favor of the board
of education.

The courts in Texas,[51] Michigan,[52] Ohio,[53] Utah[54] and
Iowa have concluded that a board of education has the
authority to prohibit married students from participating in
extracurricular activities. Although legal marriage is
sanctioned by the law and is consistent with public policy,
most school boards justify their restrictive policies as being
necessary for efficient management of the schools. The
increase in dropout rates and the undesirable influence over
unmarried pupils are frequently give as reasons for such
regulations.

In an advisory opinion by the Supreme Court of
Michigan[55] in a moot case, four of the justices in a 4-3-1
decision presented a view which might receive judicial notice
in the future. They said that denying married students the
right to participate in extracurricular activities was not a
responsible exercise of school board authority, and that the
action was arbitrary and unreasonable for no other reason
than the fact that they were married. An authoritative answer
to this question of law does not exist; it still remains for the
courts to establish a sound legal principle in this regard.

---

[51] Kissick v. Garland Independ. Sch. Dist., 330 SW(2d) 708 (Tex, 1959).

[52] Cochrane v. Board of Ed. of the Messick Consol. Sch. Dist., 360 Mich 390,
103 NW(2d) 596 (1960).

[53] State ex rel. Baker v.Stevenson,27OhioOp(2d)223,189 NE(2d)181(1962).

[54] Starkey v. Board of Ed. of Davis County Sch. Dist., 14 Utah(2d) 227, 381
P(2d) 718 (1963).

[55] Cochrane v. Board of Ed. of the Messick Consol. Sch. Dist., supra n. 52.

Chapter 4

LEGAL AUTHORITY OF ATHLETIC
ASSOCIATIONS TO CONTROL
EXTRACURRICULAR ACTIVITIES

§4.1   Influence of voluntary associations

The influence of voluntary associations over extra-curricular activities in public schools, particularly inter-scholastic athletics, is extensive. There exists in every state and the District of Columbia a high school athletic association which supervises athletics, and, in some states, regulates forensic, dramatic, and literary activities. [1]

The objectives of the various athletic associations are similar, the purpose of the Connecticut Interscholastic Athletic Conference being typical:

> The purpose of this Conference shall be to provide a central, voluntary, nonprofit organization through which the public secondary schools of the state may co-operate for the following ends: [2]

1.   To develop intelligent recognition of the place of athletics and sports in the education of our youth
2.   To establish and unify policies of administration in interscholastic athletics and sports

---

[1] Virginia High School League Handbook, Charlottesville, Va.: University of Virginia, 1963, pp. 81-101. (Other states in which a similar situation exists are Mississippi, Nebraska, North Dakota, South Carolina, and Washington).
[2] Connecticut Interscholastic Athletic Conference, Constitution and By-Laws, Wethersfield, Connecticut: Connecticut Interscholastic Athletic Conference, 1964.

3. To offer a system that will provide for equitable competition
4. To encourage the organization of recreational athletics and play for all students as an integral part of the educational program
5. To assist member schools in securing competent officials
6. To organize a force of opinion to keep interscholastic athletics within proper bounds, that will expressly encourage all that is honorable, sportsmanlike, and gentlemanly in all branches of athletic sports.

All of the state associations except that of Texas are members of the National Federation of State High School Athletic Associations. Approximately 19,500 public and private schools, representing about 8,830,000 pupils, are affiliated with the national federation by virtue of being members of their respective state associations.

The activities of the National Federation are based on the belief [that] strong state and national high school athletic organizations are necessary to protect the athletic interests of the high schools, to promote an ever increasing growth of a type of interscholastic athletics which is educational in both objective and method and which can be justified as an integral part of the high school curriculum, and to protect high school boys from exploitation for purposes having no educational implications. To accomplish these things, it is necessary for high school men to exercise teamwork on a nationwide scale. [3]

Since an adverse court decision rendered against a high school association in one state might have persuasive influence in another state, the national federation has devised a type of legal insurance. The member associations are united to give aid to any high school association which might become involved in state supreme court case.

---

[3] National Federation of State High School Athletic Associations, 1964-1965 Handbook, Chicago: National Federation of State High School Athletic Associations, 1964, p. 8.

The Mutual Legal Aid Pact permits each state association to purchase sets of the briefs and related materials which are used in connection with defense against court action. From the amounts realized from the purchase of such material, a fund is maintained and reasonable amounts are allocated to aid in defraying legal expense in defending the right to enforce regulations. By action of the National Federation Council, money received for this fund is administered as a part of the Federation general fund. Bookkeeping entries indicate how much of the general fund is available for legal aid at any given time. The amount of such aid for any association is determined by the Federation Executive Committee after studying all of the available facts. [4]

Most litigation involving high school associations has arisen as a result of a plaintiff's challenge of some eligibility or contest rule. Some of the lower courts have rendered judgment adverse to the association: "[t]emporary injuncations or adverse lower court rulings have occurred in twelve states. In each case, the injunction has been dissolved after a hearing or the adverse decision has been reversed by a higher court." [5]

High school associations are unique in their operations. By supervising interscholastic activities they assume a responsibility which legally belongs to a governmental unit: the board of education acting as an agent of the state. The existence of control over high school athletics by nongovernmental organizations was recognized by the attorney general of Ohio in an opinion given in 1933:

Interscholastic athletics is oftentimes conducted by organizations separate and apart from the regular school authorities. These organizations are sometimes incorporated as corporations for profit. More often, perhaps, they consist of mere voluntary associations composed of the principal of the school and some of the instructors, and

---

[4] Id., p. 41.
[5] Id., p. 41.

occassionally, outsiders who are interested in athletics become members of such organizations. [6]

Officials of high school associations are also aware of the restrictive controls their organizations exert over the public school activities programs:

> The [Athletic] Conference is a liability to the same degree that any cooperative enterprise imposes responsibilities on its members, and limits their freedom of action. No high school is obliged to belong but once having joined, it is subject to the rules and regulations of the organization. [7]

It is an established legal principle that the board of education has the authority to control the entire school program, curricular and extracurricular. But school boards also have the authority to permit their schools to join high school associations, [8] thereby relinquishing a portion of their control over the extracurricular program by agreeing to abide by the constituion and by-laws of the association.

Most high school athletic associations have the genuine interest of the students at heart, and do not desire to interfere with decisions not theirs to make. This philosophy is expressed in the preamble to the constitution of the Wyoming High School Activities Association:

> Recognizing the educative value of interscholastic activities, we voluntarily agree to unite in this Association to regulate, control and enjoy the greatest benefits to be derived from participation in them. It is not our desire to interfere in any manner whatsoever with the local autonomy of schools, but rather to be devoted to the elimination of excesses, and abuses, of over-enthusiastic promotion which accompanies unrestricted interscholastic

[6] Opinions of the Attorney General of Ohio, 1933, Vol. 1, No. 635, pp. 552-59.

[7] Why a CIAC? Wethersfield, Conn.: Connecticut Interscholastic Athletic Conference, pamphlet.

[8] Colorado High School Activities Assn. v. Uncomphagre Broadcasting Co., 300 P(2d) 968 (1956); State v. Judges of Court of Common Pleas, 19 OhioOp(2d) 52, 181 NE(2d) 262 (1962).

activities, and we are resolved to foster desirable outcomes through the Constitution, rules, and interpretation of the rules of this Association. [9]

State legislatures rarely place restrictions on the activities of voluntary associations. However, the South Dakota legislature recently passed a law which forbade the South Dakota High School Interscholastic Athletic Association from restricting membership in its organization to accredited public schools of the state. The law provides for the extension of membership to all accredited schools in the state of South Dakota, both public and private. [10]

Likewise, the courts seldom become involved in the activities of voluntary associations, but recently a federal court order was signed for the merger of the two high school athletic associations in Alabama. Previously the two associations, one white and one Negro, scheduled games only with members of their own association. The court order provides for the extension of integration beyond the public school classrooms to inter scholastic athletics. [10a] States which still have separate high school athletic associations are Louisiana, Mississippi, and South Carolina. [10b]

Before discussing the legal nature of high school athletic associations by examining specific cases, it is proper to review the law of voluntary associations in general.

§ 4.2   Law of voluntary associations

"An 'association' is a body of persons acting together . . . for the protection of some common enterprise." [11] Unlike a corporation which is a legal entity through franchise, an association is a creature of contract and has no

---

[9] Wyoming High School Activities Association Official Handbook, Cheyenne, Wyoming: WHSAA, Preamble of Constitution, p. 1.

[10] Richard Sabers, "Constitutionality of the South Dakota Statute Making All Accredited High Schools Eligible for Membership in SDHSIAA," South Dakota Law Review, 10 (Spring 1965), pp. 102-119.

[10a] Education U.S.A.: A Special Weekly Report on Educational Affairs, Washington, D.C.: National School Public Relations Association, April 15, 1968, p. 182. (This case was unavailable in the National Reporter System at press time.)

[10b] Id., p. 182.

[11] 7 Corpus Juris Secundum, Associations, Section 26, p. 68.

legal entity apart from the individuals comprising it. Although the terms "association" and "corporation" are sometimes used synonymously, " . . . particularly for corporations not formed for profit," [12] the meaning of the word "association" is usually restricted to unincorporated societies.

Unless specific statutory provisions exist, the organization of an association is the result of a contract of the associates and is expressed in a written document, the constitution. [13] The constitution of an association defines the rights and duties of the members [14] and can be of whatever character the members desire so long as it does not conflict with public policy, the general welfare, and the constitutions of the state and federal governments.

Generally, a member of an association may be suspended or expelled for a constitutional violation or for failure to comply with rules and regulations. The courts will uphold an association in its right to suspend or expel a member, even if the regulation providing for such action is unreasonable. [15] Any member, upon joining a voluntary association, assents to its rules and regulations and is bound by the agreement. [16]

When an issue does arise, a member should exhaust all remedies within the association before suing in court, [17] for the courts will interfere in internal association affairs [18] only if "law and justice so require," [19] as in the case of a violation of property rights.

An association, in order to sue, must bring action in the names of the members, unless statutes permit designated officers to sue in the association's behalf. [20] The same procedure must be followed when an association is sued. "An unincorporated association cannot, in the absence of statutes,

---

[12] 6 American Jurisprudence (2d), Associations, Section 2, p. 431.
[13] 7 Corpus Juris Secundum, Associations, Section 3, pp. 24-25.
[14] State of North Dakota v. North Central Assn., 23 FSupp 694; 99 F(2d) 697 (1938).
[15] Ibid.
[16] Gray v. Ferris, 230 NY 416, 245 NYS 230 (1930).
[17] State of North Dakota v. North Central Assn., supra n. 14.
[18] Gray v. Ferris, 230 NY 416, 245 NYS 230 (1930).
[19] 7 Corpus Juris Secundum, Associations, Section 34, p. 80.
[20] Gray v. Ferris, supra n. 18.

be sued in its society or company name, but all members must be made parties, since such bodies have, in the absence of statute, no legal entity distinct from that of their membership." [21]

Of particular interest in this Chapter are the high school athletic associations which supervise interscholastic athletics. Although there are few cases dealing with the legal status of high school associations, those which do exist involve the authority of these associations to prohibit athletes from participating in interscholastic athletics, the authority to suspend member schools from the association, thus preventing them from participating in the interscholastic athletic program, and the regulation of contracts dealing with the school activities program. Litigation usually results from an athlete being declared ineligible for interscholastic participation, or from an alleged violation by a school of a rule or regulation of the association for which the penalty is suspension.

§ 4.3   Authority of high school athletic associations to prohibit students from participating in interscholastic athletic contests

The first case, in which the authority of an athletic association to enforce eligibility rules for high school athletes was tested, occured in Oklahoma. [22] The board of control of the Oklahoma High School Athletic Association disqualified a group of football players at Holdenville, Oklahoma, who were rewarded with small football charms by admiring fans. The footballs were gold in color and had cost no more than two or three dollars each.

The acceptance of these charms by the members of the football team constituted a violation of the following athletic rule: "Only one athletic award of more than $1.00 in value, other than medals or trophies and cloth, felt or chenille athletic letters may be made to a student participating in interscholastic athletics." Because of this violation the athletic association prohibited the football players from participating in athletic contests between member schools for

---

[21] 7 Corpus Juris Secundum, Associations, Section 36, p. 89.
[22] Morris v. Roberts, 183 Okla 359, 82 P(2d) 1023 (1938).

one year. Even after the boys gave back the footballs action was not suspended, for, according to the judgment of the board of control, the acceptance completed the violation.

Billy Roberts, one of the football players, brought suit against the board of control of the athletic association by contending that the action taken against him was erroneous and arbitrary. He desired a writ of mandamus to compel the board of control to annul its order.

The Supreme Court of Oklahoma failed to see how the board of control could have acted arbitrarily since the only question of discretion was whether those footballs were awards.

The court said that there was nothing unlawful in any of the association's rules or in the provision investing final authority in the board of control. Each school by joining in association agreed to obey the rules and accept as final the authority given by the members to the officers of the association. The court said:

> . . . [W]hen adopted rules, acquiesced in by all, gave them [the officers] the power of final decision, such decisions should not ordinarily be reviewed by the courts and vacated by a writ of mandamus.
>
> . . . .
>
> The courts generally should leave the final authority in the athletic official or board, with whom that authority is placed by those who had authority to make the rules and authorized the method of application and enforcement.

In regard to individual rights the court said that the plaintiff had " . . . many rights as a citizen and as a high school student, but that he . . . [had] no vested right in 'eligibility' as dealt with at such great length in the rules of the Oklahoma High School Athletic Association." The board of control was therefore upheld in its decision to suspend for one year the group of high school athletes who violated the association rule.

The dissenting opinion of Justice Davison is worthy of notice because of several significant points raised. He said that there was justification for judicial interference in this case because " . . . of the field in which this association operates and its monopolistic influences upon high school athletics in this state." Since the vast majority of the high schools of Oklahoma belonged to this one association, ineligibility to participate in interscholastic competition between member teams practically prohibited an ineligible athlete from participating in high school athletics—an important segment of the public secondary school program. " . . . [W]hen a high school student of this state is, by action of the Association, forbidden to participate in athletic contests, his opportunities are greatly restricted in an important field recognized to be an integral part of his education."

Another reason given by Justice Davison in favor of judicial interference was the position of the athletic association to exert control over a field which was primarily the concern of the state and in which the general public had an interest. He said: "The courts may well shirk a corollary duty by refusing to interfere with a voluntary association which in one important field has so entwined itself with the public school system as to exercise a controlling influence."

A similar case came before the Indiana Supreme Court after the high school athletic association of that state declared two high school basketball players ineligible for interscholastic competition.[23] The two basketball players were brothers who, after moving from Illinois, enrolled in Shields High School, Seymour, Indiana. Shortly thereafter the Indiana High School Athletic Association ruled that Shields High School could not use the two new athletes as members of its competitive athletic teams, specifically basketball, under the association's eligibility rules.

The excluded athletes brought action in the Jackson Circuit Court for a restraining order and injunction to enjoin members of the athletic association from enforcing its orders. An injunction was also sought to prevent Shields High School from obeying the athletic association. After the Jackson Circuit Court issued a restraining order against the officials of the athletic association a change of venue was taken to the Lawrence Circuit Court.

---

[23] State v. Lawrence Circuit Court, 240 Ind 114, 162 NE(2d) 250 (1959).

The athletic association officials contended that they were acting within their powers and that the court had no authority to restrain and enjoin them from carrying out the rules and regulations of the association. The Lawrence Circuit Court asserted that it had jurisdication in this case because the athletic association had interfered with the plaintiffs' rights, guaranteed by the Indiana constitution and statutes, to attend public school ". . . and to utilize the study and training including physical training and athletics. . ."

The Supreme Court of Indiana said that no rule or regulation of the association interfered with the plaintiffs' right to pursue a course of study and training available and provided by law. The remaining question the court had to answer was: Did the plaintiffs' right to go to public school and receive education and training include such activities as interscholastic sports? Since this question had never been decided in the courts of the state, the Indiana Supreme Court looked to other jurisdictions for assistance. Citing *Morris* v. *Roberts.* [24] the court ruled " . . . that the right of plaintiffs under the Indiana Constitution and statutes to go to the public schools and receive education and training cannot properly be said to include interscholastic sports and games." The Lawrence Circuit Court was without jurisdication in this case, and the Indiana High School Athletic Association rule of eligibility was held valid and enforceable and free from court interference.

In 1962, the Supreme Court of Ohio upheld a ruling of the Ohio High School Athletic Association which declared two athletes ineligible for interscholastic athletics, and suspended a high school from interscholastic football competition for one year. [25]

Litigation developed as a result of an alleged violation of Section 2 of Rule 8 of the athletic association's rules:

The use of undue influence by any person connected or not connected with the school to secure or to retain a

---

[24] Morris v. Roberts, 183 Okla 359, 82 P(2d) 1023 (1938).

[25] State v. Judges of Court of Common Pleas, 19 OhioOp(2d) 52, 181 NE(2d) 262 (1962). See also Lee O. Garber, "At Last: A Big Step Toward High School Athletics Clean-Up—With Court Approval," The Nation's Schools LXX (December, 1962), p. 44.

student or the parents of a student shall cause the student to be ineligible and shall jeopardize the standing of the school in the association.

On August 28, 1961, the superintendent of schools of Portsmouth, Ohio, wrote a letter to the commissioner of the Ohio High School Athletic Association in which he said that "Canton McKinley [High School] stole one of our football players." The commissioner, upon conducting a thorough investigation, discovered that the moving of a family with two football players from Portsmouth to Canton was in violation of the association's "undue influence" rule. Subsequently, the board of control rendered the two boys ineligible for interscholastic athletic participation, and Canton McKinley High School was suspended from interscholastic football competition for the 1962-63 season. Appeal of the ruling was permitted, and a full rehearing was held on November 8, 1961, at which time the former action was affirmed.

The two athletes and the high school did not bring suit, but the prosecuting attorney of Stark County brought action in the court of common pleas for the issuance of a temporary order restraining and enjoining the members of the board of control, all officers of the association, and forty-five member boards of education from enforcing the order suspending Canton McKinley High School from interscholastic football.

In seeking a writ of prohibition from the Supreme Court of Ohio against the lower court order, the relators alleged that the prosecuting attorney of Stark County had no reason to sue because (1) he was not a member of the association and had no interest or right in its management and (2) the action did not involve any property rights of the prosecuting attorney and therefore the court of common pleas had no jurisdiction over the matter. The relators contended that in the absence of a writ of prohibition issued against the court of common pleas, they would be unable to perform their official duties under the rules of their association. This situation they said would be harmful to the cause of "wholesome amateur athletics."

The respondents filed a demurrer to the petition which raised the question: Does a school board have the authority to permit one of its schools to become a member of a voluntary association whose purpose is to promote wholesome amateur athletics among its members? The court answered this question in the affirmative by citing the constitutional and statutory authority of school boards to make rules and regulations for the government of schools. Boards of education may authorize individual schools to join voluntary associations such as the Ohio High School Athletic Association.

In relation to the association itself, the court concluded that it had no judicial authority to interfere with internal affairs of a voluntary association so long as all activities were in keeping with the constitution and rules and regulations subscribed to by the members. The respondents did not allege any wrongdoing on the part of the athletic association, but complained that the penalty was too harsh because the students of Canton McKinley High School would be denied the opportunity to see their school play football, and the school band would be denied the opportunity to perform before the public at football games. In answering this complaint the court said:

> These assertions do not constitute grounds for the issuance of a court injunction.

> The penalty imposed by the association is indeed harsh and most severe. However, in the absence of mistake, fraud, collusion or arbitrariness, the decision of the association will be accepted by the court.

In answer to the respondents' contention that government regulation of interscholastic athletics was necessary, the court praised the work of the Ohio High School Athletic Association for its " . . . excellent task in the supervision and control of interscholastic athletics for more than half a century. . . ." The court was of the opinion that there was nothing of "judicial notice" to indicate that governmental officials could do a better job of supervising interscholastic activities than the athletic association had done.

In granting the writ of prohibition against the court of common pleas, the Supreme Court of Ohio stressed its strong conviction that the courts should not interfere with the internal affairs of the Ohio High School Athletic Association, lest interscholastic athletics would be destroyed:

> This court recognizes that a writ of prohibition is an extraordinary remedy. However, if the restraining order of the Court of Common Pleas of Stark County is allowed to stand, the whole system of supervision and control of interscholastic athletics in Ohio will be in jeopardy. This situation would continue for an indefinite period of time, during which there would be no effective supervision or control, and as a result of this, such a damaging blow to clean athletics at the secondary school level could occur that interscholastic competition, as we know it, would be destroyed.

In an Illinois case a similar decision was rendered when the authority of an athletic association was challenged by an athlete who was declared ineligible for competitive sports.[26]

According to a rule of the Illinois High School Association an athlete whose nineteenth birthday occurred on or before December 10, was ineligible for interscholastic sports after December 11. Jasper Lee Robinson claimed his nineteenth birthday was on December 24, 1962, but the athletic association, after a thorough investigation, concluded that Robinson's birthday occurred prior to December 10, and that he was ineligible to participate in interscholastic athletics.

Upon being declared ineligible by the board of education, Robinson brought suit in the circuit court of Winnebago County against the athletic association and the board of education for an order restraining the defendants from declaring him ineligible for competitive sports and for a writ of mandamus compelling them to declare him eligible to play for Auburn Senior High School. After hearing the case, the circuit court concluded that the plaintiff's birthday occurred after December 10, and enjoined the defendants to declare the plaintiff eligible for interscholastic sports.

---

[26] Robinson v. Illinois High School Assn., 45 IllApp(2d) 277, 195 NE(2d) 38 (1963).

The case was then appealed to the appellate court of Illinois which reversed the circuit court by saying:

> . . . [T]here is no evidence of fraud, collusion or that the defendants acted unreasonably, arbitrarily, or capriciously. A determination of the ineligibility of plaintiff to play interschool basketball was made by those in whom the constitution, by-laws, and rules of the Illinois High School Association vested the power and duty to make that determination.

In a decision, dealing primarily on the question of jurisdiction and venue, the Supreme Court of Appeals of West Virginia upheld the judgment of the West Virginia Secondary Schools Activities Commission in its choice of the two teams to play the state Class AA football championship game. [27]

The West Virginia Secondary Schools Activities Commission, a voluntary unincorporated organization for the supervision and control of interscholastic athletics, operates under a constitution and regularly adopted by-laws. The president, vice-president, and treasurer constitute a board of appeals which has the authority to appoint deputy board members and an executive secretary. Although questions of eligibility and rule violations may be submitted to deputy board members and the executive secretary, both officers of which are appointed by the board of appeals, the decision of the board of appeals is always final.

Under the provisions of the by-laws, the board of appeals is authorized to adopt a point rating system for determining which teams are eligible to participate in the state championship games for the various school classifications.

In 1957, three Class AA teams were undefeated: Big Creek High School, Weir High School, and West Fairmont High School. When Weir High School and West Fairmont High School were declared the eligible teams by the executive secretary and the board of control of the activities commission, two members of the Big Creek High School team brought suit in the circuit court of Mercer County against the

---

[27] West Virginia Secondary Sch. Activities Comm. v. Wagner, 102 SE(2d) 901 (WVa, 1958).

commission, the regional deputy and resident of Mercer County, Melvin McClain, and the three members of the board of appeals, all of whom resided outside of Mercer County. The plaintiffs contended that the Big Creek High School team, not the Weir High School team, was eligible to compete in the Class AA championship game, and that the commission violated its by-laws by not submitting the dispute to the regional deputy.

Upon the issuance of an injunction by Judge Wagner of the circuit court against the defendants to prevent them from declaring the Big Creek High School team ineligible for participation in the Class AA championship game, the commission, by the members of the board of appeals, filed a proceeding with the Supreme Court of Appeals of West Virginia for a writ of prohibition to prevent the trial court from proceeding further with the suit. The supreme court ordered the operation of the injunction suspended until after a hearing, thus permitting the championship game to be played as scheduled by the teams designated by the activities commission.

Following the hearing the supreme court ruled that the bill of complaint in the suit in equity did not state a valid cause of action against the West Virginia Secondary School Activities Commission. A voluntary unincorporated association cannot be sued in its name as a separate legal entity in the courts of the state. And Melvin McClain, the only resident defendant who was sued in Mercer County, had no necessary part in the suit, since neither the constitution nor the by-laws of the commission vested power or authority in him to declare any team ineligible for championship competition. The only cause of action, if any, was against the members of the board of appeals in whom was vested the authority to determine eligibility for championship competition, but since none of these defendants were residents of Mercer County and were not served with process in that county, cause of action did not arise against them.

In awarding the writ sought by the board of appeals of the commission the court said:

. . . [T]he petitioners are entitled to the writ for which

they pray for the reason that venue of the suit in equity does not exist in Mercer County and the circuit court does not have jurisdiction of the necessary parties to the suit. . . .

The authority of high school athletic associations to determine the eligibility of high school athletes in member schools and teams to participate in interscholastic athletics has been upheld by the courts. So long as the athletic associations abide by their constitutions and rules and regulations, the courts will not, in the absence of a violation of property rights, interfere with the internal operation of the association.

§ 4.4   Authority of high school athletic associations to regulate contractual obligations of member schools

The first significant case in which an athletic association and a member school were involved in a dispute over the terms of a contract occurred in Florida.[28] In June, 1939, Palmetto High School made a contract with Sarasota High School for a football game which was played in the autumn of 1939. On the reverse side of the contract it was written that Palmetto High School would have the choice of giving one of the following contracts for the 1940 football season: (1) the same contract as 1939, (2) a $200 guarantee, or (3) a fifty-fifty split on the gate. In April, 1940, Sarasota High School severed relations with Palmetto High School and there developed a controversy over the playing of a 1940 football game.

A regulation of the Florida High School Athletic Association prohibited the cancellation of contracts without mutual consent. In case of disagreement the dispute was to be referred to the executive secretary of the athletic association for adjudication. The executive secretary's decision, or that of the executive commission in case of appeal, was to be final and the decree binding. This dispute between the two member schools was submitted to the executive secretary of the athletic association. Upon examination of the case, the

---

28 Sult v. Gilbert, 148 Fla 31, 3 S(2d) 729 (1941).

executive secretary concluded that the contract provided for only the 1939 game. The terms on the reverse side of the contract intended to provide for a gamc in 1940, but, not being covered in the contract as originally executed, they could not be enforced. In accordance with the regulation of the athletic association, Palmetto High School apparently accepted the decision, for an appeal was not sought.

However, in October, 1940, Palmetto High School filed a bill of complaint in the circuit court praying that Sarasota High School be required to play football with them in November of that year. The chancellor ruled in favor of Sarasota High School by declaring the contract unenforceable. Immediately the executive secretary of the Florida High School Athletic Association cited Palmetto High School to show reason why it should not be suspended from the association for failing to accept the executive secretary's decision as final. After a full hearing the executive secretary held that Palmetto High School did not accept his decision and was to be suspended from the association for one year. Upon appeal, the executive commission affirmed the executive secretary's ruling.

Palmetto High School then filed another bill of complaint which, among other things, prayed that the school not be suspended from membership in the association. The court found the suspension order regular and in compliance with the constitution of the association, but issued a temporary restraining order enjoining suspension until several contracted games were played. The case then went by appeal to the Supreme Court of Florida. The court dealt with the question: Is the order of the executive secretary as affirmed by the executive commission suspending Palmetto High School from the association for one year valid and enforceable? Palmetto High School contended that (1) the executive secretary and the executive commission had no authority to adjudicate the contract, (2) that the association constitution did not authorize suspension for violation, and (3) that valuable property rights were involved that warranted court action to enforce. The court reiterated the established legal principle that the consitution of a voluntary association subscribed to by the members upon joining becomes a contract and members can be suspended or expelled for insubordination, as was the situation in this case. In regard to property rights the court said:

> The constitution of the Florida High School Athletic Association shows that it is a voluntary nonprofit organization. When Palmetto High School was a member of the association, it had a right to make contracts with member schools for athletic meets. The loss of this right was all that was lost by the suspension and that being the case, we find no showing of a contractual or property right that would authorize the courts to interfere. It was purely an internal affair of the association and there is no showing of mistake, fraud, collusion, or arbitrariness in the proceedings.

Although the athletic association had a legal right to enforce its rules and regulations without judicial interference, the court said " . . . that under all the circumstances the penalty in this case was too harsh but was not more than was authorized."

In a 1952 Texas case, an athletic association was prohibited from interfering with the performance of a member school's contract which involved property rights. [29]

Midwestern University had a contract with the Wichita Falls Independent School District to use Coyote Stadium, a public school facility, in Wichita Falls. The university wanted to use the stadium to play an all-star football game, an event which was prohibited by Rule 34 of the regulations of the University Interscholastic League of which the Wichita Falls Independent School District was a member. Rule 34 prohibited the use of any public school personnel or facilities " . . . in any all-star game in which one or more of the competing teams . . . [was] composed of a player or players who, during the previous school year, were members of the high school football team." Any member school violating this rule was subject to prohibition or suspension.

---

[29] University Interscholastic League v. Midwestern University, 250 SW(2d) 587 (Tex, 1952).

To obtain use of the stadium, Midwestern University sued the University Interscholastic League to restrain enforcement of the rule prohibiting use of public school facilities for all-star games, and the public school district to compel performance of the contract. The district court of Wichita County issued a mandatory injunction in favor of the university. The court said that:

> . . . all persons, firms, corporations and voluntary associations, including the University Interscholastic League, are permanently enjoined from in any way interfering with the performance of such contract or using its performance as a basis for sanctions against the Wichita Falls Independent School District or any of its member schools.

The University Interscholastic League appealed to the court of civil appeals of Texas upon several points of error, the main one being Rule 34 which prohibited the use of the public school stadium for an all-star football game. In the opinion of the court this rule was ineffective to the subject matter of the case: the use of property belonging to the public schools. The main concern was whether the athletic league had the authority to regulate the use of public school property. The dilemma of this situation was pointed out by the court by citing a passage of the appellees' brief:

> If the trustees carry out their public duty to maintain competitive athletics and join the "Interscholastic League Football Plan,"–their discretion to control the use of their public school property is restricted.

> If they exercise their lawful rights of control over their public properties, even by honoring possible previous contractual commitments,–then the Interscholastic League . . . will deprive their public charges (students) of the privilege of competitive athletics.

In sustaining the permanent injunction against the University Interscholastic League the court said:

> We find that the League is without authority to enforce restrictions provided in its Rule 34. The duties of an

athletic director, coach, teacher or administrator of a public school in this state can only be regulated by the officers of the school system of the state in accordance with the provisions of statutes pertaining to this subject.

The University Interscholastic League then appealed the case to the Supreme Court of Texas.[30] The supreme court ruled that Midwestern University had no right under its contract to use Coyote Stadium for games other than those played by its own team. The court then considered the question: Did the action of the school district trustees in authorizing membership in the league and agreeing to abide by its rules interfere with the performance of their duties to the public? After the president of the board of school trustees and the superintendent of schools testified under oath that they felt it a part of their duty in office to see that their high school was a member of the league, the court concluded that the enforcement of Rule 34 by the league did not interfere with the trustees' performance of duties to the public, and upheld the right of the league to enforce Rule 34, thus prohibiting Midwestern University from holding the all-star football game in Coyote Stadium.

In a Colorado case, the state high school activities association was permitted to require member schools to charge private radio stations fees for the privilege of broadcasting football games.[31]

The Colorado High School Activities Association adopted a schedule of fees for broadcasting high school athletic events. Half of the fee was to be paid to the school and half to the activities association. When a broadcasting company was charged $12.50 for broadcasting rights for a football game, it filed suit against the activities association because it prohibited free radio broadcasts of high school games. The broadcasting company contended that the operation of the activities association was illegal because it dictated policies to high schools, and that the charging of fees for the privilege of

[30] University Interscholastic League v. Midwestern University, 255 SW(2d) 177 (Tex, 1953).
[31] Colorado High School Activities Assn. v. Uncompahgre Broadcasting Co., 300 P(2d) 968 (Colo, 1956).

broadcasting high school games was a violation of the rights of the broadcasters.

In a temporary restraining order against the activities association, the district court of Delta County ruled that the association had no authority to force public high schools to collect broadcast fees. By declaring the association regulation unconstitutional the trial court rendered void the fees contract between the activities association and the several schools of Colorado. The court also said that the payment of annual dues and the agreement to other assessments by member schools was a violation of the rights of local school boards.

When the case came before the Supreme Court of Colorado the school district argued that the regulation of relationships between the school district and the activities association was beyond the scope of issues the broadcasting company could call upon the trial court to determine. They also contended that the trial court erred in concluding that school membership in the activities association was an encroachment upon control of educational activities by school boards.

In arriving at a decision favorable to the school district and the activities association, the supreme court upheld the right of a public school to charge fees, denied the trial court the authority to declare void contracts between the activities association and other schools not party to the action, and prohibited the broadcasting company from challenging the manner in which district funds were distributed in other than a taxpayers' action. By reversing the decision of the lower court the Supreme Court of Colorado confirmed the constitutionality of the activities association to regulate and control extracurricular activities.

High school athletic associations have the right to control contracts made by member schools so long as provisions to do so are present in the constitution or by-laws.

§ 4.5 Summary

In every state and the District of Columbia there exists a voluntary high school association which supervises and controls extracurricular activities, interscholastic athletics in par-

ticular. All of these state associations except that of Texas
are members of the National Federation of State High School
Athletic Associations. The purpose of this national organization is to promote teamwork among the state organizations
to further the cause of wholesome interscholastic activities
among the secondary schools of the nation. The national
federation has also devised a type of legal insurance under
which all state associations support a member in a lawsuit
which reaches the state supreme court. All state associations
have a direct interest in lawsuits of this nature because of the
persuasive influence the decision might have in future cases in
which the same or similar question might be dealt with by
the courts of other states.

Voluntary associations have no legal entity apart from
their members, and they must, in the absence of statutory
provisions, sue and be sued in the names of their members.
Before a school sues the association of which it is a member,
all remedies of appeal within the association must be exhausted.[32] Even then, the courts will not interfere in the
internal affairs of a voluntary association unless law and
justice so require, as in a case where property rights are
violated.

School boards have the authority to permit schools under
their direction to join high school athletic associations.[33] By
becoming a member of a high school association a school
assents to abide by the constitution and rules and regulations
of the association.[34] Any violation of the constitution or
rules and regulations of a high school association may result
in the member's suspension or expulsion from the association.[35]

The courts do not have the authority to interfere with the
operations of high school associations so long as all internal

[32] State of North Dakota v. North Central Assn., 23 FSupp 694; 99 F(2d)
697 (ND, 1938).
[33] Colorado High School Activities Assn., v. Uncompahgre Broadcasting Co.,
300 P(2d) 968 (Colo, 1956); State v. Judges of Court of Common Pleas, 19 Ohio
Op(2d) 52, 181 NE(2d) 262 (1962).
[34] Morris v. Roberts, 183 Okla 359, 82 P(2d) 1023; Sult v. Gilbert, 148 Fla
31, 3 S(2d) 729 (1941).
[35] Sult v. Gilbert, 148 Fla 31, 3 S(2d) 729 (1941); State v. Judges of Court of
Common Pleas, 19 OhioOp(2d) 52, 181 NE(2d) 262 (1962).

activities are conducted according to the constitution and
rules and regulations of the association and no property
rights are violated.[36] Athletic associations have been upheld
by the courts in their regulation of contracts made by member schools so long as provisions for such regulations were
present in the constitution or by-laws of the organization.[37]
In the absence of mistake, fraud, collusion, or arbitrariness
the courts have upheld athletic associations in their awarding
of harsh penalties for the violation of rules and regulations so
long as these penalties were provided for in the constitution
or by-laws.[38]

Because of their supervision and control of extracurricular
activities, high school athletic and activity associations appear
to operate in an extralegal capacity, outside the framework
of the state governments which are responsible for public
education. However, there are no significant cases in which a
high school association has received an adverse decision in the
courts of record when the authority of the association to
control public school activities was challenged.

---

[36] Morris v. Roberts, 183 Okla 359, 82 P(2d) 1023; Sult v. Gilbert, 148 Fla
31, 3 S(2d) 729 (1941); State v. Lawrence Circuit Court, 240 Ind 114, 162
NE(2d) 250 (1959); State v. Judges of Court of Common Pleas, 19 OhioOp(2d)
52, 181 NE(2d) 262 (1962); Robinson v. Illinois High School Assn., 45
IllApp(2d) 277, 195 NE(2d) 38 (1963).

[37] Sult v. Gilbert, 148 Fla 31, 3 So(2d) 729 (1941), University Interscholastic
League v. Midwestern University, 250 SW(2d) 587 (Tex, 1952), 255 SW(2d) 177
(Tex, 1953), Colorado High School Activities Association v. Uncompahgre
Broadcasting Co., 300 P(2d) 968 (Colo, 1956).

[38] Sult v. Gilbert, 148 Fla 31, 3 S(2d) 729 (1941), State v. Judges of Court of
Common Pleas, 19 OhioOp(2d) 52, 181 NE(2d) 262 (1962).

Chapter 5

LEGAL CONSIDERATIONS INVOLVING
TEACHERS ASSIGNED TO
EXTRACURRICULAR ACTIVITIES

§ 5.1   Reasons for litigation

Litigation involving extracurricular personnel usually comes about as a result of disagreements pertaining to teachers' contracts or because teachers challenge the authority of school officials to assign them extracurricular duties not specifically mentioned in their contracts of employment. The assignment of extracurricular duties without extra compensation frequently creates dissatisfaction among teachers which, if unsatisfactorily resolved, sometimes culminates in litigation.

The majority of the cases concerning teachers' extracurricular duties involve the contracts of athletic coaches and the authority of school boards to assign to teachers, without additional compensation, extra duties totally unrelated to their teaching fields.

§ 5.2   Legal implications involving the contracts of athletic coaches

Regulations governing the relations of a board of education with its teachers in force at the time of employment are, by implication, read into the teacher's contract. [1] "All persons dealing with the board of [education] are bound by its rules and regulations, . . . whether or not they are actually cognizant of such rules and regulations." [2]

---

[1] Edwards, The Courts and The Public Schools, p. 482.

[2] Underwood v. Board of Public Ed. for City of Savannah and Chatham County, 25 GaApp 634, 104 SE 90 (1920).

Teachers are also bound to obey all reasonable rules and regulations adopted after they have signed their contracts, [3] and the willful refusal of a teacher to obey reasonable rules and regulations of the employing board of education is insubordination [4] for which a teacher can be dismissed. In the field of extracurricular activities, for example, a board of education was upheld by the court in discharging a teacher of physical education and coach of athletics for lack of cooperation and physical abuse of pupils. [5]

Although school districts have the authority to employ athletic coaches who, like all other teachers, are bound by the rules and regulations of the school, all states do not provide tenure protection in relation to coaching duties after a probationary period of satisfactory employment, as is common in academic fields.

The Supreme Judicial Court of Massachusetts held that a city school committee alone had the authority to contract with and hire an athletic coach without the approval of the mayor. [6]

In Massachusetts there is a statute which sets forth the conditions under which a school committee may employ a coach:

The [school] committee may contract to employ athletic coaches for periods not in excess of three years. The provisions . . . relative to tenure shall not apply to such athletic coaches, unless they are otherwise entitled to tenure. [7]

The duly elected school committee of the city of Salem appointed David R. Gavin to the position of football coach for a period of three years at a salary of $2,500 per annum, with the right, at his option, to renew the contract for an

[3] School City of East Chicago v. Sigler, 219 Ind 9, 36 NE(2d) 760 (1941).
[4] State ex rel. Steele v. Board of Ed. of Fairfield, 252 Ala 254, 40 S(2d) 689 (1949).
[5] Anderson v. Board of Ed. of Sch. Dist. No. 70, Winnebago Co., 10 IllApp(2d) 63, 134 NE(2d) 28 (1956).
[6] School Committee of Salem v. Gavin, 333 Mass 632, 132 NE(2d) 396 (1956).
[7] Annotated Laws of Massachusetts, Vol. 2B, Chap. 71, Sec. 47A.

additional year at the same salary. This contract, executed between the school committee and Gavin, did not bear the signature of the mayor of Salem, a statutory requirement for contracts in excess of $1,000 in plan B cities such as Salem.

Before the three years had expired the school committee voted to declare the position of football coach vacant. The school committee then sought declaratory judgment to determine the validity of the contract. The superior court decreed the contract to be invalid because it did not bear the mayor's signature. In response to this decision, Gavin appealed to the Supreme Judicial Court of Massachusetts. The supreme court, upholding the supremacy of the school committee to make this contract, said in part:

> We are of the opinion that the contract here is one which the school committee alone had the power to make . . . In granting to school committees this broad supervisory control over athletics the Legislature must have intended to place such matters as the selection of athletic coaches and the power to contract with them exclusively under the [school] committee's control.

The court pointed out that this power of the school committee would be seriously thwarted if the approval of the mayor were necessary for executing valid contracts.

As was illustrated by the statute mentioned in this case, athletic coaches do not always enjoy the protection of the state tenure laws in relation to their extracurricular duties, even though such duties might be specifically mentioned in their contracts of employment. This fact was brought out in an Illinois case. [8]

On August 8, 1946, C. Donald Betebenner, a teacher and athletic coach at the West Salem Community High School, was notified by the board of education that his duties as a teacher had ceased with them and that he would receive no subsequent salary. Betebenner informed the board of education that he claimed employment for the academic year 1946-1947 under the provisions of the Illinois Teacher

---

[8] Betebenner v. Board of Ed. of West Salem Community High Sch. Dist. No. 201, Edwards Co., 336 IllApp 448, 84 NE(2d) 569 (1949).

Tenure Act, but upon reporting to school on September 2, 1946, he was again informed that there were no duties for him to perform then or in the future. In accordance with their announced policy, the board of education refused to reinstate Betebenner for the year 1946-1947.

On August 11, 1947, Betebenner began action in the circuit court of Edwards County on the ground that he was entitled to the benefit of contractual continued service under the Teacher Tenure Act. The plaintiff sought a writ of mandamus to compel the defendant board of education to employ him as a full-time teacher for the academic year 1947-1948 at a salary of $2,300 and to pay him the same amount, together with legal interest, for the previous school year. The circuit court, concluding that the plaintiff was on tenure, granted the writ of mandamus ordering that he be reinstated at a salary of $2,300 and that he receive $2,300 plus interest for back salary.

From this decision the board of education appealed to the Supreme Court of Illinois. The appellants, in addition to contending that the appellee did not have tenure status, said that the circuit court erred in reinstating this teacher at a salary of $2,300. The board of education said that if reinstatement of the appellee was in order he should have received only $1,900, since his coaching duties were contracted for on a basis separate from his teaching duties. He had also requested to be relieved of coaching duties, due to health, and no definite conclusion had been reached in regard to his possible assignment.

The supreme court ruled that the appellee had tenure status and should be reinstated as a teacher, but that he was ineligible to receive the $400 for coaching duties under the tenure act:

> We do not interpret the tenure act to mean that contractual continued service status will attach to extracurricular services when they are contracted for separately, at a specified amount. Furthermore, the board could, in response to the request of petitioner, relieve him of coaching duties with the right to apply the $400.00 to whomever was selected to perform those duties. Hence the writ

should have ordered petitioner reinstated at a salary of $1,900.

The court did not award the appellee $2,300 plus interest for the previous year, for the sum, due to his request to be relieved of coaching duties, had not been established and was therefore not properly recoverable in mandamus.

In 1962, a Florida court came to a similar conclusion by ruling that rights of tenure applied only to employment as teacher pursuant to the certificate issued by the state and did not extend to the right of reemployment as an athletic coach. [9]

Walter Slater, a teacher certified in business education, was assigned the duty of serving as coach and athletic director of the football team in St. Augustine High School. He was also employed on a year-to-year basis as the director of the summer recreational program. Although he was not certified in physical education, he received $1,000 per annum for his coaching duties and $890 for his summer employment, in addition to his regular salary for classroom teaching.

After three years of satisfactory service Slater was granted a continuing contract by the local board of education, in accordance with the state statute providing for teacher tenure.

In the spring of 1961, Slater informed the county school superintendent that he intended to resign his position to accept a similar position elsewhere. The same information was released to the press and received widespread publicity. Because of the situation created by the coach's announced intention to resign, the board of education passed a resolution requesting him to submit his formal resignation or be reassigned as a full time teacher to perform such duties as the school administration designated. When he refused to resign he was assigned full teaching duties and was relieved of his position of coach and athletic director of the football team and of his summer position of director of the recreational program.

---

[9] State ex rel. Slater v. Smith, 142 S(2d) 767 (Fla, 1962).

In response to the action of the school board, Slater insti-
tuted a mandamus proceeding; he claimed that his continuing
contract of employment conferred upon him the right to
continue as coach and athletic director of the football team
as well as a member of the staff in the summer recreational
program. The circuit court of St. Johns County denied the
plaintiff the writ of mandamus which he sought, on the
ground that continuing contracts in the public schools in
Florida apply only to the position for which the teacher is
certified. Upon appeal to the district court of appeal of
Florida, this decision of the trial court was affirmed:

> It is our conclusion that appellant's rights of tenure
> apply only to his employment as a teacher for which he
> held a certificate issued by the State Department of Educa-
> tion. Such tenure under the continuing contract of
> employment held by appellant does not extend to the
> right of re-employment as a coach or athletics director.
> For the same reason appellant's tenure does not extend to
> the right of being re-employed on a continuing basis in the
> summer recreational program . . . .

The court also ruled against the appellant's claim that he
could not be relieved of such duties in the absence of a public
hearing which authorizes dismissal only for good reason.
Since the rights of tenure in this case did not cover the duties
of which the appellant was relieved, the court held that the
board of education could not violate any rights of tenure and
was therefore not required to hold a public hearing.

Chief Justice Caroll, dissenting in part, disagreed with the
majority of the court in their ruling that a teacher was not
protected by the tenure act in duties other than those teaching fields for which he was certified by the state. He contended that an athletic coach is, because of the nature of his
duties, a member of the instructional personnel as defined in
the tenure act. In support of his opinion that an athletic
coach is a teacher he said:

> In many of the competitive sports conducted under the
> public school program, and especially in football, there is
> much to be taught by the member of the staff in charge to

the participating students. Not only must the rules of football be taught by the football coach but also measures to be taken in connection with safety and good health. The alert coach also will no doubt spend much time in teaching the students the rules of good sportsmanship—which will be of much importance to them in their lives after graduation from school. In this aspect a football coach is not only a teacher but a teacher of some of the most important things that can be learned in a school program. From the record before us it appears to me that Slater is in this category of "teacher."

In Missouri, a state in which school boards may not dismiss teachers, a court of appeals permitted a school board to relieve a teacher and athletic coach of his duties after he submitted his resignation, effective at the termination of his contract, and then abandoned his contract.[10]

Mark Burns, the plaintiff in this case, was employed by the Fulton School District No. 58 to teach general business, physical education, and coach football and track for the academic year 1960-1961. On March 30, 1961, he submitted his resignation, effective upon the fulfillment of his contract. Thereafter he made public statements critical of the athletic program and the disciplinary problems of the local schools.

The board of education, after an investigation, resolved to reprimand Burns officially by relieving him of all his duties in the school system. The plaintiff then asked for a public hearing and requested full payment of his remaining salary. The board of education did not hold a public hearing but did pay the plaintiff, early in April, the balance of salary due him.

There were no further developments until May 12, 1961, when the plaintiff filed in the circuit court of Callaway County a petition for injunction to restrain the defendants from interfering with the performance of his duties for the remainder of the school year. The trial court denied the plea, and the plaintiff appealed to the Kansas City Court of Appeals. This court also ruled in favor of the board of education by saying that the advance payments of salary requested

10 Burns v. Harris, 358 SW(2d) 257 (Mo, 1962).

and received by the appellant was evidence enough to regard the contract as terminated or abandoned. Therefore the court declined to issue a writ of injunction against the board of education to compel them to permit the appellant to resume his duties of teacher and athletic coach.

In several instances the additional annual compensation received by teachers for coaching athletics, not specifically mentioned in their regular contracts of employment, has been challenged as not being part of the highest annual salary used for the determination of pension benefits.

The law division of the superior court of New Jersey said that a high school football coach who had been given an honorarium each year at the conclusion of the football season could not add this amount to his regular salary when applying for his pension to the State Teacher's Pension and Annuity Fund.[11]

William Matthews, a former high school teacher and football coach, challenged the board of education for refusing to pay him a pension of $3,050 per annum instead of the $2,700 which he was receiving. Under the pension law he was entitled to 50 percent of his highest salary. He therefore contended that he should receive an additional $350, for he had received from the board of education a $700 honorarium for his last year of coaching, from which was deducted pension benefits. But the court ruled that " . . . the plaintiff ha[d] no rights to pension beyond that of half of . . . his contract salary. . . " Upon appeal to the Appellate Division of the Superior Court of New Jersey this decision was affirmed on the ground that gratuitous payments could not be included in the total amount from which the amount of pension could be determined.[12]

The Supreme Judicial Court of Massachusetts ruled that additional compensation received by a teacher for performing coaching duties was part of his total annual salary;[13] in this

---

11 Matthews v. Board of Ed. of Irvington, Essex Co., 29 NJSuper 232, 102 A(2d) 110 (1953).
12 Matthews v. Board of Ed. of Irvington, Essex Co., 31 NJSuper 292, 106 A(2d) 346 (1954).
13 Murphy v. Boston, 337 Mass 560, 150 NE(2d) 542 (1958).

instance, however, the additional pay was provided for in the salary schedule.

William Murphy, a retiring teacher and athletic coach, was entitled to 65 percent of his highest annual compensation received while teaching the grade held by him at the time of his retirement. Upon application for retirement benefits, the mayor of Boston informed him that his highest annual compensation was $6,056 and not $7,856, for $1,800 paid for two-hundred days of coaching was not a part of his pay which could be used for determining his retirement benefits. The superior court of Suffolk County decided in favor of the mayor and the case was appealed to the supreme judicial court. This court had to decide whether the appellant had held two grades since he had two contracts: one for his regular teaching duties and one for coaching duties. The court, in deciding in favor of the teacher, said:

> We think that whether the plaintiff held one grade or two . . . , the work was so related that he was entitled to be retired from what he was doing and to have the highest annual compensation under both types of appointment stand as the base for his retirement pay.

The value of extracurricular activities has been recognized by both educators and judges, yet there is a tendency to regard coaching duties as being separate from the teachers' regular classroom responsibilities. This phenomenon is illustrated by the litigation discussed in this section regarding tenure and pension benefits for athletic coaches.

§ 5.3   Authority of school officials to assign extracurricular duties to teachers

The widespread acceptance of the value of extracurricular activities in the public school program has created some problems in personnel administration for school officials. These activities, for all practical purposes, must be supervised by teachers. And school administrators have the responsibility of selecting the teachers to be assigned various extracurricular activities. This task is usually no significant problem in the assignment of activity sponsors, for the school authorities generally have the authority to assign to teachers any duties for which they are qualified on the basis of their teaching certificate. It would not be unreasonable for school authorities to request a music teacher to direct the school band or orchestra; similarly, a chemistry teacher could be expected to sponsor the school science club. However, a problem sometimes arises when teachers are assigned duties such as supervising student spectators at athletic contests, collecting tickets for various school events, or chaperoning school social functions—duties totally unrelated to their classroom teaching assignments.

Although extracurricular activities are generally accepted as an important part of the total school program, many athletic and club activities are conducted after school hours and on Saturdays. Because of the extra time involved in certain extracurricular assignments, some teachers have requested additional compensation for their services.

According to a study conducted by the research division of the National Education Association for the school year 1962-1963, "[t]he practice of giving extra pay for extra services is widespread." [14] The extent to which teachers sponsoring athletics, instrumental and vocal music, dramatic productions, school publications, and debating were compensated was illustrated by this study, but no mention was made of extra compensation for club advisors or for duties such as supervision of students or collecting tickets at athletic events. It is possible that some schools do compensate for these responsibilities but were not indicated in this study because only school systems which had specific provisions mentioned in their salary schedules were analyzed. Although only 210 of the 563 schools studied included within their regular salary schedules supplementary schedules for extracurricular duties, ". . . it is safe to conclude that in the majority of school systems there are informal provisions for extra pay not included in the salary schedule." [15]

Although state legislatures may define the duties of teachers, "[u]sually the statutory provisions pertaining to

14 "Extra Pay for Extra Duties," National Education Association Research Bulletin, XLI (May, 1963), pp. 50-51.
15 Id., pp. 50-51.

duties of teachers are stated in broad terms with express or implied delegation of authority to boards of education to determine the assignment of duties for teachers." [16]

In some instances contracts of employment are specific in prescribing extraclass assignments of teachers, but frequently " . . . the authority of school administrators to make extra assignments is stated in such general and vague terms that the school principal is compelled to exercise his discretion in the matter." [17] When teachers believe that school administrators have exceeded their legal authority to assign duties either specified or implied in the contract of employment, they sometimes, in the absence of a satisfactory administrative settlement, bring the dispute before the courts for adjudication.

The courts have been quite consistent in holding that teachers are bound by *express* provisions in the contract. Even where the contractual obligations are only *implied*, the courts have been reluctant to interfere with the school officials' exercise of discretion. Therefore there is not likely to be judicial disapproval of school officials' reading into the contract the right to assign extra-classroom duties to teachers, providing they are within statutory limits and reasonable in amount and nature. [18]

The legal status of extra assignments applied equally to tenure as well as non-tenure teachers, but the teachers usually wait until they receive permanent tenure before challenging the authority of school administrators to assign them extra duties. [19]

Because the courts are reluctant to interfere with the internal management of the school, a dispute is frequently adjudicated, not on the question of the school administrator's authority to make an extra assignment but on the reasonableness of the assignment. [20] The following questions

---

[16] E. C. Bolmeier, "Legality of Extra Assignments for Teachers" in Law and the School Principal, Cincinnati: The W. H. Anderson Co., 1961, p. 193.
[17] Id., p. 194.
[18] Id., p. 195.
[19] Id., p. 195.
[20] Id., pp. 195-96.

are considered by the courts in determining the reasonableness of the assignment.[21]

1. Does the assignment require excessive hours beyond the normal teaching period?
2. Does the assignment have some relation to the teacher's interests, abilities, and certification?
3. Is the assignment made because of its intended benefit to the pupils?
4. Is the assignment discriminatory?
5. Is the assignment professional in nature?

"In spite of the many extra assignments which classroom teachers are asked to perform and the many objections made thereto, few of these disputes have been so serious as to result in litigation."[22]

In response to the question of the legality of extracurricular assignments for which no additional compensation is received the assistant attorney general of Kentucky said: ". . . [I]t is the opinion of this office that a teacher may be assigned 'extra duties' without 'extra compensation' as long as said 'extra duties' are not unreasonable, arbitrary, or discriminatory."[23]

When giving his response to the question whether the supplemented salary for additional duties set forth by statute intended to include extracurricular student activities the Attorney General of Ohio said:[24]

[I]t is my opinion that supervision of extra-curricular student activities properly may be included within the "additional duties" provided by statute. In view of our present concept of a school system, which concept includes many activities supervised by the school beyond the teaching of classroom subjects, it is reasonable to assume that the General Assembly intended that the teachers supervising such activities might be compensated.

---

21 Id., p. 196.
22 Kentucky Attorney General Opinions 1960-1964, OAG 63-106, p. 2-1020.
23 Id., p. 2-1020.
24 Opinions of the Attorney General of Ohio, 1952, No. 1080, p. 11-13.

The attorney general also contended that it is within the discretion of the board of education to decide whether the activities for which extra compensation is given are proper ones to be subsidized by the public schools. "The board's decision on such a question can be upset only if it has abused its discretion by providing pay for an activity that has no reasonable connection with a proper school system." [25]

The first case to set a precedent in relation to extra-curricular assignments of public school teachers occurred in Pennsylvania. [26] William Ganaposki, a public school teacher, was employed by the city of Farrell where he taught history, civics, physical education, and coached athletics for many years. Under his most recent contract he was instructor of physical education and coached football and basketball. When the school authorities relieved him of his football coaching duties, he refused to coach basketball. Because of his action the board of education chose not to re-elect Ganaposki to the teaching staff. After receiving notice of his removal, Ganaposki brought suit against the board of education in the court of common pleas of Mercer County and upon receiving an adverse decision appealed to the Supreme Court of Pennsylvania.

The appellant contended that under the proper construction of the word "teach" as used in his contract, the school officials were without authority to refuse him re-election. He said that his contract said "teach," and since no reference was made to coaching, he could not legally be relieved of his position so long as his physical education assignment was conducted satisfactorily. The court, therefore, had to answer this question: Can the word "teach" be construed to include teaching duties?

In the opinion of the court " . . . the discretion of the school authorities . . . [was] absolute, under the contract, to assign the teacher regardless of prior understandings before his contract was entered into." The board of education had the power to assign teachers duties for which they were properly qualified and certified. The court reasoned that

---

[25] Id., p. 11-13.
[26] Appeal of Ganaposki, 332 Pa 550, 2 A(2d) 742 (1938).

" . . . [t]here can be no doubt that a comprehensive definition of 'teaching' physical education embraces all fields of athletics including coaching football and basketball." The statutes support this line of reasoning because no law exists which provides either for teachers in specific athletics or for hiring of coaches who have no teaching certificates.

In rendering a judgment favorable to the board of education, the supreme court said:

> [The] appellant was a qualified instructor in physical education and was assigned to coaching duties. It was a proper assignment, within the power of the school authorities. When a professional employe is regularly employed to "teach," thereafter he may be assigned such teaching duties for which he is qualified as the board may direct, and if he refuses to obey such instructions he is guilty of "willful and persistent negligence" for which he may be dismissed.
>
> . . . .
>
> There was sufficient evidence that appellant was assigned, under his contract, to the duties which he refused and willfully neglected to perform, and the school board acted properly in dismissing him after notice and hearing.

Another dispute involving a similar question came before the Supreme Court of Rhode Island for adjudication.[27] There was a clause in the teachers' contract which read as follows: "You shall perform all work in a satisfactory manner, including such extra-curricular activities as may be assigned." Joseph E. McKeon, in behalf of himself and other teachers, asked the school committee to clarify this provision in the teachers' contract relating to extracurricular assignments. He said that the contract was vague and lacked mutuality, for certain of the extra-curricular duties would be mandatory, others voluntary, and still others mandatory but would command extra compensation. When the school committee refused to comply with the wishes of the teachers, an appeal was taken to the director of education of Rhode Island.

---

[27] McKeon v. Warwick School Committee, 75 A(2d) 313 (RI, 1950).

The teachers petitioned the director of education to compel the school committee to clarify the teachers' contract and make it comply with the Teacher Tenure Law. When the director of education refused to do so the teachers referred his decision to a justice of the supreme court. In the opinion of Chief Justice Flynn " . . . the form of appointment or contract submitted to the appellants to be signed . . . [did] not of itself violate any expressed or implied provisions of the Teacher Tenure Law." Therefore, there was no question for the director of education to decide, because the school committee had committed no wrong.

In deciding in favor of the school committee Chief Justice Flynn concluded:

> Unless and until appellants are required to perform extracurricular activities under rules and regulations which violate the law or exceed the school committee's proper powers, any claim that appellants are aggrieved persons under the present statute is without legal foundation . . .
> In the circumstances, therefore, it is my judgment that the objectives of the appellants are without merit and the decision of the director of education should be affirmed.

In a New York case the court reaffirmed the authority of the board of education to assign extracurricular duties to teachers if these duties were related to the teacher's training and certification and were not unreasonable. [28]

The board of education passed a resolution which contained the following provisions relating to extracurricular activities:

1. Every teacher is required to give service outside of regular classroom instruction in the performance of functions which are the essential duties of any teacher.
2. There is an area of teacher service which is important to the well rounded educational program of the students, but in which teachers participate in varied ways according to their interests, capabilities and school

---

[28] Parrish v. Moss, 106 NYS(2d) 577 (NY, 1951).

programs. The principal has the responsibility and duty to see to it that these activities are carried on. The principal may assign beyond the specified hours of classroom instruction, and the teacher is required to render such service.

3. In the assignment of teachers to these activities, principals are directed to see to it that in so far as is practicable, such assignments are equitably distributed.

The petitioners argued that this regulation was invalid because, among other things, it provided for an unlawful delegation of powers to the principal to fix duties and hours of teachers without providing for adequate protection for the teachers. In deciding this question, the court ruled that under the rules and regulations of the board of education the principal had the full responsibility for conducting the extracurricular program of the school. The board of education, through its principals in this case, had the authority to assign extracurricular duties to teachers even if the assignments had to be conducted after the close of the school day. It was pointed out by the court that the duties assigned to the teachers must be related to their fields of certification. For example, a physical education teacher could be expected to coach athletics; likewise, an English teacher could be required to supervise dramatic productions and student publications. The court also pointed out that the board of education was not required to pay additional compensation for these services so long as they were related to the teacher's classroom work, but " . . . where the service . . . [was] not part of the duty of the teachers, there . . . [was] nothing to prevent the board [of education] from arranging for such extra service and paying for the same in its discretion."

The court upheld the board of education in its right to fix teachers' hours by citing *Matter of Shapiro* v. *Board of Education*:[29]

Our conclusion is that in a matter within the tutelage of the internal management of the board of education and

---

[29] Matter of Shapiro v. Board of Ed. 250 AppDiv 57, 293 NYS 603 (1937).

the discipline of the working hours, their length, or its lack prescribed for the various teaching staffs, the courts ought not to interfere with the authority primarily responsible for the conduct of the schools unless there is palpable discrimination or arbitrary action detrimental to the individual or class.

The assignment of a teacher to collect tickets at an athletic event was declared an improper assignment for a professional employee by a Pennsylvania court. [30]

Todd Coronway, a social studies and physical science teacher at Lansdowne High School, was advised that he would have to serve without compensation as a ticket collector at a football game. When he informed the school authorities that he refused to perform the assignment without additional compensation, he was notified by them that he was not legally entitled to extra compensation for extracurricular assignments and that refusal to perform such duties would be regarded as willful and persistent negligence. The board of education made it clear that the policy of making such assignments was done in the past and would continue in the future.

In a suit brought before the court of common pleas of Delaware County, Coronway prayed for both a preliminary and a permanent injunction restraining the defendant board of education from compelling him and other teachers to perform extracurricular activities without reasonable additional compensation, and from compelling them to work or teach longer hours than permitted by law. [31]

The plaintiff received an adverse decision because he failed to exhaust all possible administrative remedies before presenting his case to the court. A statute requires that such a dispute be submitted to the state superintendent of public instruction for adjudication prior to an appeal to the courts.

Coronway then gave the board of education notice that he considered taking tickets a demotion in salary and type of position and demanded a hearing. The board of school direc-

---

[30] Appeal of Coronway, No. 785, 38 DelCoRep 406 (Pa, 1951).
[31] Coronway v. Lansdowne Sch. Dist. No. 706, 37 DelCoRep 412 (Pa, 1950).

tors held a series of five hearings to consider Coronway's charge but unanimously decided against him. Following the statutory requirements for resolving such cases, Coronway then appealed to the state superintendent of public instruction, who immediately dismissed the appeal and sustained the board of education.

Since all administrative remedies for settling the dispute were exhausted, Coronway took his case to the court of common pleas. [32] The court, deciding in favor of the plaintiff, did not fail to overlook the precedent set in *Appeal of Ganaposki, supra,* in which it was held that a school board could assign teachers extra duties which were directly related to their teaching assignments:

> The assignment of teachers to supervise . . . [extracurricular] activities is well within the powers of the school boards. However, we cannot see how an assignment to collect tickets at a football game can be considered in such a category. Were the petitioner assigned to sit with the students and in a cheering section to help to inculcate in them the attributes of loyalty and good sportsmanship, we might regard such an assignment as having some direct relation to the education of his pupils but the assignment to sit beside a gate and collect tickets bears no such relation. It is a task which any adult could perform and can only be motivated by the desire of the School Board to cut down the expenses of the game. We feel that such an assignment is not within the field which a teacher must perform and to require him to do so is a demotion in type of position.

The court reversed the decision of the state superintendent of public instruction by ruling that the assignment in question was not " . . . within the scope of the teaching duties of a professional employee."

Several years later a case involving a similar question came before the courts of California. [33] Edward G. McGrath, a teacher at Sacramento High School, objected to the assigned

---

[32] Appeal of Coronway, No. 785, 38 DelCoRep 406 (Pa, 1951).
[33] McGrath v. Burkhard, 131 CalApp(2d) 376, 280 P(2d) 864 (1955).

non-class activities involved in supervision of school football and basketball games. Male teachers were required to attend six games per year, three each of football and basketball. Their duties consisted of protecting the general welfare of the students by maintaining order in the stands and reporting any disturbances to the police officers also in attendance. Under this policy, which was carried out for years, assignments were made impartially and the requests of teachers for particular games were honored in as many cases as possible.

The plaintiff sought declaratory relief on the grounds that these nonclass assignments did not fall within the scope of his duties and that they were unprofessional in nature. He asked the superior court of Sacramento County to declare:

1. The rights and duties under the contract of employment.
2. That nonclassroom work was not within the scope of employment.
3. That plaintiff should not be assigned duties on a teaching day which require more than eight hours per day to perform completely.
4. That if more than eight hours may be assigned, the court should declare the number of hours per day plaintiff is obliged to perform under contract.
5. That no duties be assigned on days for which he is not paid, i.e. Saturdays, holidays, and most nonteaching days.

After a trial in which the defendant board of education denied the allegation made by the plaintiff, the court concluded (1) that the board of education had the right to assign plaintiff any teaching duties within the scope of his credentials provided that it did not reduce his rank or grade position held during probationary service; (2) that the board of education had the right to assign plaintiff to assist in the supervision of athletic and social activities conducted under the name or auspices of the Sacramento High School so long as such assignments were made impartially and without discrimination; and (3) that since the plaintiff's employment was professional in nature, the services could not be arbitrarily measured but depended upon the reasonable needs of the school program, so long as the hours of service were not unreasonable.

McGrath then presented his case to the court of appeals by contending that he was under no contractual obligation in regard to athletic assignments, and if so obliged the assignments were unreasonable because they were in the nature of police work, unprofessional, foreign to his field of instruction, and imposed unreasonable hours upon him.

The court, in its ruling against the appellant, said in part:

> Teachers are engaged in a professional employment. Their salaries and hours of employment are fixed with due regard to their professional status and are not fixed upon the same basis as those of day laborers. The worth of a teacher is not measured in terms of a specific sum of money per hour. A teacher expects to and does perform a service. If that service from time to time requires additional hours of work, . . . a teacher expects to and does put in the extra hours, without thought of measuring his or her compensation in terms of a given sum of money per hour. A teacher's duties and obligations to students and the community are not satisfied by closing the classroom door at the conclusion of a class. The direction and supervision of extracurricular activities are an important part of his duties. All of his duties are taken into consideration in his contract for employment at the annual salary. All of this is, of course, subject to the test of reasonableness. It does not appear that six of these athletic assignments in an entire year are unreasonable, nor that the hours of such assignments are unreasonable under the circumstances. What is reasonable must necessarily depend upon the facts of the situation and the teachers are protected in that regard by the appropriate administrative and judicial procedure. Supervising the students and being present to protect their welfare at school athletic and social activities, conducted under the name and auspices of the school, is within the scope of the contract and such assignments are proper so long as they are distributed impartially, they are reasonable in number and hours of duty, and each teacher has his share of such duty.

It was the consensus of the court that the school authorities had a right under the law to determine that such extracurricular assignments should be performed by the teachers.

The Supreme Court of Pennsylvania recently ruled that a teacher may be assigned extra duties only if the activity to which he is assigned is related to the school program. [34]

George L. Pease, Jr., a social studies teacher, was assigned to supervise a boys' bowling club which met once each week away from school at a local bowling center. The board of education sanctioned the club, but in no way supported the group in which membership was voluntary. The school system paid none of the expenses, there was no intramural or interscholastic bowling team, and the faculty sponsor did not coach or instruct the group. Providing a teacher for disciplinary purposes was the only connection between the school district and the bowling club.

After Pease was notified of this assignment he informed the high school principal and the superintendent of schools that he would not accept this duty, for it was beneath his dignity and not appropriate to a teacher. He did not indicate a willingness to accept another extracurricular assignment. The board of education gave him a legal hearing and then dismissed him " . . . on the grounds of incompetency, persistent negligence and persistent and willful violation of school laws."

Pease appealed to the state superintendent of public instruction, who sustained his appeal and directed his reinstatement as a teacher on the ground that the board of education had no reasonable rules for distributing extracurricular assignments. Therefore, the state superintendent ruled that for this reason Pease " . . . was under no contractual obligation to accept the assignment and thus the charge of incompetency on this basis . . . [could not] be sustained."

The case came before the Supreme Court of Pennsylvania after the court of common pleas of Erie County reversed the state superintendent's decision. The majority of the court agreed with the decision reached by the state superintendent,

[34] Pease v. Millcreek Tp. Sch. Dist., 195 A(2d) 104 (Pa, 1963).

but dealt with what they thought to be the real question of the case: "Was. . . the bowling activity to which Pease was assigned by the board [of education] . . . so related to the school program as to justify the board [of education], under . . . the School Code [to] . . . make this assignment?" Answering this question in the negative, the court said in part:

School teachers must realize that they are subject to assignment by the school board to any activity directly related to the school program; classroom duties in school hours do not constitute all their duties. On the other hand, school boards must realize that their power of assignment of school teachers to extracurricular duties is not without limitation and restriction; under . . . [the law an] activity to which a school teacher is assigned must be related to the school program and the assignment must be fairly and reasonably made.

The court therefore concluded that the board of education exceeded its authority in making this assignment because the bowling club was not related to the school program.

§ 5.4   Summary

Litigation involving the teachers responsible for conducting extracurricular activities stems from two sources: disputes pertaining to teachers' contracts, especially those of athletic coaches, and teachers challenging the authority of boards of education to assign them extra duties unrelated to their teaching fields or for which they receive no extra compensation.

Boards of education have the authority to hire athletic coaches to conduct the extracurricular athletics program..[35] Although athletic coaches are subject to the same rules and regulations under their contracts as are other teachers, their athletic duties are not always included under the teacher tenure laws. In Massachusetts there is a statute which permits

---

[35] School Committee of Salem v. Gavin, 333 Mass 632, 132 NE(2d) 396 (1956).

school committees to hire coaches for no longer than a three-year period. [36]

The Illinois Supreme Court ruled that contractual continued service did not attach to extracurricular coaching duties when they were contracted for separately. [37] The district court of appeal of Florida came to a similar conclusion by declaring that the rights of tenure applied only to the subject area in which a teacher was certified by the state. [38] A business education teacher who was relieved of coaching duties had no legal basis to bring action against the board of education. The school board was not required by law to hold a public hearing, for they violated no rights of tenure by reassigning the teacher and coach to full-time teaching duties.

School boards in Missouri cannot dismiss teachers, but the Kansas City Court of Appeals upheld a school board which relieved a teacher of his teaching and coaching duties after he had submitted his resignation and had been paid his complete salary, even though the school year had not ended. [39]

In two instances supplementary compensation for coaching athletics was challenged as not being a part of the athletic coach's total salary which could be used for determining pension benefits. The New Jersey courts ruled that an honorarium received for coaching athletics was not part of a teacher's total salary used for determining the amount of pension to be paid to him upon retirement. [40] The Supreme Judicial Court of Massachusetts ruled that extra compensation for coaching duties, provided for in the regular salary schedule, was part of a coach's total salary under the pension law. [41]

Many extracurricular activities meet during out-of-school hours, either after school or on Saturdays. This situation creates a problem for the school administrators whose

---

[36] Annotated Laws of Massachusetts, Vol. 2B, Chap. 71, Sec. 47A.

[37] Betebenner v. Board of Ed. of West Salem Community High Sch. Dist. No. 201, Edwards Co., 336 IllApp 448, 84 NE(2d) 569 (1949).

[38] State ex rel. Slater v. Smith, 142 S(2d) 767 (Fla, 1962).

[39] Burns v. Harris, 358 SW(2d) 257 (Mo, 1962).

[40] Matthews v. Board of Ed. of Irvington, Essex Co., 29 NJSuper 232, 102 A(2d) 110 (1953); 31 NJSuper 292, 106 A(2d) 346 (1954).

[41] Murphy v. Boston, 337 Mass 560, 150 NE(2d) 542 (1958).

responsibility it is to assign teachers to supervise these activities. Problems most frequently arise when teachers are assigned, often without compensation, duties foreign to their teaching assignments, such as supervising student spectators at athletic games, collecting tickets for various school events, and chaperoning school social functions.

The Pennsylvania Supreme Court ruled that a board of education had the authority to assign teachers duties for which they were properly qualified and certified, and their failure to perform such duties would make them guilty of willful and persistent negligence for which they could be dismissed.[42] The Supreme Court of Rhode Island declared that a school committee had the authority to assign extracurricular duties to its teachers so long as the rules and regulations did not violate the general statutes and teacher tenure law or were not in excess of the school committee's proper power.[43]

In a New York case the court said that a board of education could fix the working hours of a teacher even to the extent of evening hours if the activity assigned was related to the teacher's field of certification.[44]

A court of common pleas in Pennsylvania declared that the assignment of a teacher to collect tickets at an athletic event was an improper assignment for a professional employee.[45] Had this teacher been assigned to supervise pupils in the cheering section, the court would have regarded the duty as one of educational significance within the authority of the board of education to assign.

A teacher in California brought suit against the board of education for assigning him supervisory duties at athletic games for which he received no extra compensation. The court ruled in favor of the school board by stating that a teacher's duties extend beyond the classroom and that such assignments, when reasonable and distributed impartially, were within the power of the board of education to assign.[46]

[42] Appeal of Ganaposki, 332 Pa 550, 2 A(2d) 742 (1938).
[43] McKeon v. Warwick School Committee, 75 A(2d) 313 (RI, 1950).
[44] Parrish v. Moss, 106 NYS(2d) 577 (1951).
[45] Appeal of Coronway, No. 785, 38 DelCoRep 406 (Pa, 1951).
[46] McGrath v. Burkhard, 131 CalApp(2d) 376, 280 P(2d) 864 (1955).

In a more recent case the Supreme Court of Pennsylvania ruled that a teacher may be assigned extra duties only if the activity to which he is assigned is related to the school program. [47] The assignment of a teacher to supervise a boys' bowling team which met at a local bowling center and which had no affiliation with the school was beyond the authority of the school board to make.

---

[47] Pease v. Millcreek Tp. Sch. Dist., 195 A(2d) 104 (Pa, 1963).

Chapter 6

TORT LIABILITY AS RELATED TO EXTRACURRICULAR ACTIVITIES

§ 6.1   The governmental immunity principle

Tort liability cases constitute the majority of the litigation relating to extracurricular activities of public schools. Accidents resulting from athletic activities, involving both participants and spectators, are the most common.

The common-law rule that school districts are generally not liable for the negligent acts of their officers, agents, and employees, in the absence of statutory provisions imposing liability on them, is well established in American jurisprudence. The legal principle of governmental immunity has been applied to school districts because they are extensions of the state government functioning in a local capacity to carry out a state responsibility—education of the children of the community.

Since school districts generally cannot be held liable for the negligent acts of their employees, the rule of *respondeat superior* does not apply in most school tort cases, and teachers and employees of the school district can be held personally liable for their negligent acts. In the area of extracurricular activities it is the athletic coach who is most vulnerable as a result of governmental immunity. Accidents occur most frequently in interscholastic athletics, and a coach who is found negligent for the injury of an athlete can be compelled to pay damages to the student.

Although the courts and legislatures of some states have modified the common-law principle of governmental immunity,[1] the majority of the school districts in the United States are immune from liability, particularly when conducting governmental functions: those activities of a strictly educational nature.

Governmental agencies, municipalities in particular, perform two functions: those which are public or governmental and those which are private or proprietary. The nature of the function being performed at the time an accident occurs determines whether or not a governmental body is liable for the negligence of its employees.

> [I]f the function exercised by the municipality at the time of the injury to the plaintiff was a governmental function there is no liability, but if the function so being exercised was a proprietary function then the municipal corporation is liable. [2]

Although school districts are quasi-municipal corporations, the distinction between governmental and proprietary acts is also applied to them by many courts.

Aware of the sovereign immunity protecting school districts in most states, numerous plaintiffs have brought suit on the ground that the board of education was engaged in a private or proprietary activity for which it could not claim immunity from liability. The duty of providing public education is a responsibility of the government and is therefore an undisputed governmental function. However, there are certain activities in which a school district might engage that the courts sometimes regard as proprietary in nature. The Supreme Court of Pennsylvania declared that a recreation

---

[1] The courts in Illinois, Michigan, Wisconsin, Minnesota, and Arizona have abrogated governmental immunity. "Save harmless" statutes which permit boards of education, themselves immune from suit, to defend their teachers who are personally liable have been passed by the legislatures of New York, New Jersey, Connecticut, Oregon, Massachusetts, and Wyoming. The states of California, Hawaii, New York, North Carolina, Alabama, and Mississippi have either abolished or modified the doctrine of governmental immunity. For a thorough discussion of tort liability and governmental immunity see: David V. Martin, "Trends in Tort Liability of School Districts as Revealed by Court Decisions," Unpublished Ed. D. Dissertation, Duke University, 1962.

[2] Delmar W. Doddridge, "Distinction Between Governmental and Proprietary Functions of Municipal Corporations," Michigan Law Review, XXIII (February, 1925), p. 333.

program, not a part of the regular school curriculum, was proprietary: [3]

> In general, . . . it has been said that if a given activity is one which a local government unit is not statutorily required to perform, or if it may also be carried on by private enterprise, or if it is used as a means of raising revenue, the function is proprietary.

The courts do not always agree which functions are proprietary and which are governmental when deciding school tort cases. "In the overwhelming majority of cases it is impossible to determine into which category a given act will fall until the courts have ruled." [4]

§ 6.2 Proprietary functions and legal liability for injuries sustained in a program of extracurricular activities

The courts must frequently determine whether a school board, by supervising an extracurricular event for which admission was charged, had conducted itself in a proprietary capacity.

The first significant case in which a court declared that an athletic contest for which admission was charged was a proprietary function occurred in Scranton, Pennsylvania, in 1949. [5]

An action for personal injuries was brought against the Scranton School District by a person who was injured in the course of attending a football game for which he paid admission. The plaintiff received injuries when the roof of a shed upon which was erected seating facilities for spectators, and upon which he was seated, collapsed. The case against the board of education was based on the plaintiff's contention that the conducting of athletic events, for which fees were collected from approximately 10,000 spectators, was a proprietary function rather than a governmental one, and that

---

[3] Morris v. School Dist. of the Tp. of Mount Lebanon, 393 Pa 633, 144 A(2d) 737 (1958).

[4] Robert R. Hamilton and Paul R. Mort, The Law and Education, Brooklyn. N.Y.: The Foundation Press Inc., 1959, p.282.

[5] Hoffman v. Scranton School Dist., 67 D&C 301 (Pa, 1949).

the school district for engaging therein was liable for harm occurring to invitees because of negligence of the school district's agents or employees. Claiming immunity from liability, the defendant board of education contended that the plaintiff failed to set forth a cause of action because a school district, as an agent of the commonwealth, is not liable for the tortious acts of its servants, agents, or employees while involved in governmental functions.

It was the task of the court to resolve the following question: May a school district, in providing for and maintaining a thorough and efficient public school system, operate for the entertainment of a large number of patrons an athletic event which, with its side concessions, approached the proportions of a commercial sports presentation?

The court declared that such an activity was not within the legitimate function of the school district:

> . . . [A] governmental function is one which is performed by some agency of government in pursuance of the duty of government to provide for the safety, health and welfare of its citizens. On the other hand, those functions are corporate or proprietary which are performed by such an agency for the convenience or comfort of the persons served by such an agency and which could as well be performed by private individuals if the agency chose not to perform them. . . .[T]o use the present situation as an . . . illustration, it is obvious that while physical education and training in games may be considered a part of the school district's governmental business, because made so by the Constitution, it is equally obvious that any private promoter in the sports field could conduct a football game between opposing teams, school or otherwise, collect admission fees therefor, provide for seating accommodations and be responsible for the protection of patrons while in his park, at least to the extent of responsibility for failure to warn them of a dangerous condition. We can see no reason why a school district should not be equally responsible, for we consider that the arrangement for such a public spectacle, desirable and interesting as it may be, is nevertheless not necessary to the business of the school

district of providing a thorough and efficient system of public schools and, therefore, not within the legitimate scope of its operation as a governmental agency.

Because the school district had engaged in an activity which the court declared to be outside of its authority, governmentally, it was held liable for the negligence alleged by the plaintiff in this case.

The Supreme Court of Arizona came to a similar conclusion by declaring that a school district by leasing its stadium had engaged in a proprietary act and that it could be held liable for injuries sustained as a result of its negligence to maintain the stadium. 6

Legal action was brought against a school district by a person who was injured while a spectator in its stadium. The plaintiff was critically injured when he fell through a railing which had been permitted to exist in a condition of disrepair. The question that the court had to answer in this case was: Is a school district which leased its stadium immune from liability for its own torts in failing to keep the stadium in repair and safe for the use of the public?

Deciding in favor of the plaintiff, the court declared that the board of education was engaged in a proprietary act over which it was not willing to extend the protection of governmental immunity. Justice Phelps, expressing the opinion of the majority of the court, said in part:

We believe that the majority of the text book writers are of the view that such a doctrine [of governmental immunity] has no application in this country especially in view of the fact that the reasons assigned by the courts for its perpetuation no longer exist. This seems to be especially true since liability insurance is available to state government and to its subdivisions for the protection of persons who may become injured as a result of a tort committed by an officer, agent or employee of government.

. . . [W]e are certainly not inclined to extend the

6 Sawaya v. Tucson High Sch. Dist. No. 1 of Pima County, 78 Ariz 389, 281 P(2d) 105 (1955).

doctrine of non-liability of governmental subdivisions any further than we are required to do.

. . . .

We hold that in leasing the stadium and receiving compensation therefor that the school district was in exercise of a proprietary function and . . . is liable for injuries sustained as a result of its negligence in the maintenance of said stadium.

Justice Windes, who disagreed with the majority of the court, expressed the following opinion in his dissent:

The general rule is that school districts act only in a governmental capacity and are not liable unless expressly authorized by statute, since the establishment and maintenance of schools is a governmental function.

. . . [F]or the promotion of the public function for which the school districts are created, the district cannot be said to have been acting in a proprietary or private capacity in making such charge.

. . . .

The charge made by . . . [the school] district is not for the private benefit of the district. It must go into the school fund and cannot be expended by the district for any purpose except educational . . . [activities] . . . . The fact that a school makes incidental charges for various activities does not convert it into a business enterprise.

The Pennsylvania Supreme Court, in a more recent tort liability case, declared that a school district which offered a summer recreation program, not part of the school curriculum and for which an admission fee was charged, was conducting a proprietary activity.[7] The school district by so doing waived its right of governmental immunity for any acts of negligence which might result therefrom. In this suit the school district was charged with the alleged negligent death of an infant girl by drowning in a swimming pool operated by

---

Morris v. School Dist. of Tp. of Mount Lebanon, 393 Pa 633, 144 A(2d) 737 (1958).

the school district and open to the general public for an admission fee. Concluding that the school district was engaged in a proprietary activity, the court rendered a decision favorable to the plaintiff. Since the recreation program was proprietary in nature the school district could not be protected by governmental immunity and was therefore liable for the negligence of its employees.

Although these three courts [8] declared that a school district may be held liable for the negligent acts of its employees when such negligence results in injuries associated with an activity which may be classified as proprietary, other courts have been unwilling to rule likewise.

In a Florida case, a woman, injured by a baseball which came through a protective screen which had been negligently permitted to deteriorate, sought damages on the theory that the board of education while conducting a proprietary activity was liable for injuries sustained as a result of negligence in the maintenance of the stadium. [9] The plaintiff cited the *Hoffman*[10] and *Sawaya* [11] cases in support of her claim, but the district court of appeal failed to be persuaded by these decisions:

> We have carefully studied the cited decisions and in all frankness must agree that they are solid support for the position which appellants here take. They completely discredit and repudiate the ancient doctrine of sovereign immunity and reject as unsound the several reasons relied upon by our Supreme Court for the settled rule which immunizes county school boards against liability for torts committed by their agents or employees. We are compelled to the view, however, that such conflict in judicial opinion does not in any manner alter the established law of this jurisdiction.

----

[8] Court of Common Pleas of Lackawana County, Pennsylvania, Supreme Court of Arizona, and the Supreme Court of Pennsylvania.

[9] Buck v. McLean, 115 S(2d) 764 (Fla, 1959).

[10] Hoffman v. Scranton School Dist., 67 D&C 301 (Pa, 1949).

[11] Sawaya v. Tucson High Sch. Dist. No. 1 of Pima County, 78 Ariz 389, 281 P(2d) 105 (1955).

The court concluded that any change in the doctrine of governmental immunity in the state of Florida would have to be made ". . . either by constitutional amendment, or by enactment of appropriate legislation, or both."

The Supreme Court of Minnesota also upheld governmental immunity when it decided a case involving a suit filed against a school district to recover damages for injuries sustained by a football player whose face was pushed in the unslaked lime which was used to mark the football field.[12] The plaintiff, whose sight was lost in one eye and greatly impaired in the other, brought action against the board of education on the ground that the use of unslaked lime to mark the football field was a negligent act which created a nuisance, for which the school district could not claim governmental immunity because the sponsoring of the game, at which admission was collected, was a permissive or nongovernmental act.

The supreme court ruled in favor of the school district by ruling that the charge made for admission did not ". . . take the district out of its educational function and convert its activity into one of a business or proprietary character."

Similarly, the Supreme Court of Montana held that the charging of admission to a basketball game by a school district was a governmental function.[13]

This action was brought by a woman who was injured when a stairway leading to a gallery for spectators collapsed. She alleged that the construction was faulty and that the stairway was not properly maintained. Pointing out that the school district was carrying out a governmental function, the court said:

A part of . . . physical training consists . . . [of] the playing of games—basket ball among others. Because some [pupils] are better able to coordinate the action of the different members of the body, they are more adept at

---

[12] Mokovich v. Independent Sch. Dist. of Virginia, No. 22, 177 Minn 446, 225 NW 292 (1929).

[13] Rhoades v. School Dist. No. 9, Roosevelt County, 115 Mont 352, 142 P(2d) 890 (1943).

playing games than are others; but with basket ball, as in other games, practice makes perfect.

It is a matter of common knowledge that, in these schools, teams are selected to play against another team or teams of the same school; and that out of all of these are selected those who have acquired the greatest proficiency, and these compose the team which represents the school in contests with teams from other schools in the same general vicinity. In striving to make the first team there is great rivalry. A spirit of emulation is developed—all of which results in a more complete development of the physical powers. Undoubtedly, one of the elements which stimulates the contestants is that they will be afforded an opportunity of exhibiting their skill in games against their fellows of the same school or against teams of a different school. This, we think, is true, not alone as it pertains to physical sports, but the same may be said of debating teams, or of band concerts, or of exhibitions of the art department of a school. The fact that a band concert is held, or an exhibition of the work of those in the art department of the school had, brings better results in each of these departments. Therefore, we conclude that the basket ball game in question was merely a part of the program of physical education of the school; and, consequently, the defendants were exercising governmental functions in connection therewith.

In regard to the plaintiff's charge that the collection of an admission fee made the activity a proprietary one, the court commented:

Little if any difference does it make whether the admission fee thus collected went into the school fund, or whether the expense of conducting this game of basket ball was paid for from general taxation. The result is the same. It advances the purpose of physical education. That is a part of the governmental functions of the school district and of its trustees.

Failing to agree with the majority of the court, Justice

Erickson, in a dissenting opinion, attacked the rule exempting school districts from tort liability:

> The rule arose . . . from the old idea that the king could do no wrong, and suit would not lie against the sovereign. The courts of this land have never agreed on any single basis why, in the absence of statute, recovery against the school district cannot be had by reason of tort. . . . Most of the states, in attempting to decrease the severity of the rule, have adopted the governmental-proprietary test. This test is an arbitrary one, but the general trend of the decisions is to declare more and more functions proprietary rather than governmental so as to allow recovery. It is now generally agreed that neither logic nor justice supports the general rule which in this case denies recovery to the person injured as in this case where she goes for entertainment to a basket ball game sponsored by a school district, while on the other hand for exactly the same injury under the same conditions she could recover if she had gone to a theatre and had been there injured.

The Supreme Court of Michigan also ruled that an athletic event for which admission was charged was not a proprietary act but a governmental one, for such an activity was part of the regular physical education program.[14]

A girl was fatally injured when she fell into a concrete ramp leading to the school warehouse while she was a paid spectator at a high school football game. The deceased girl's administratrix based the right to recover against the school district on its negligence to safeguard, protect, and light the ramp; the maintenance of a dangerous nuisance; and the breach of its contract for failing to provide the girl with a safe place to travel while she was a paid attendant at the football game.

The school district claimed immunity on the ground that it was a quasi-municipal corporation—an agency of the state—for which there was no recovery for negligence on the part of its employees; that the girl, not a student of the high school,

---

[14] Watson v. School Dist. of Bay City, 324 Mich 1, 36 NW(2d) 195 (1949).

was guilty of contributory negligence; and that the ramp area, adjacent to the parking lot, was not a part of the athletic field to which the public was invited.

The plaintiff, in support of the claim of school district liability, contended that those who were not students or otherwise connected with the school were not benefited by the physical education program and that their only interest was to attend the contest, thus making it a commercial operation for profit which removed the protection of governmental immunity. Defending athletic events as a legitimate part of the physical education program, the school board claimed that admission charges were only incidental and that football contests were therefore not commercial in nature. Agreeing with the defendant board of education, the court held that the school district, by sponsoring an athletic contest for which admission was charged, was not liable for injuries because it was conducting a governmental activity and not a proprietary one. The court was convinced that interscholastic athletics are definitely a part of the regular physical education program.

The Supreme Court of Tennessee upheld governmental immunity of school districts because, in its opinion, they could conduct themselves in no other than a governmental capacity. [15]

Donald F. Reed, the plaintiff, brought action against Rhea County and the board of education to recover for injuries received by him while witnessing a high school football game as a paying spectator. He was injured when the bleachers upon which he was seated collapsed. His allegation was that the bleacher seats collapsed because they were negligently constructed, and that the school district was liable because it was maintaining a private enterprise for profit. Rhea County contended that it was not liable because it had acted in a governmental capacity and was therefore protected by the doctrine of governmental immunity.

The court, supporting the county's contention, concluded that the school district was not acting in a proprietary capac-

---

[15] Reed v. Rhea County, 189 Tenn 247, 225 SW(2d) 49 (1949).

ity. In fact, it said that a school district's entire activities were governmental:

> The duties of a County Board of Education are limited to the operation of the schools. This is a governmental function. Therefore, in legal contemplation there is no such thing as such a Board [of Education] acting in a proprietary capacity for private gain.

The problem of proprietary and governmental activities of a school district in relation to athletic contests for which admission was charged became the central question in another case which occurred in New Jersey in 1951.[16] A woman brought action against the board of education to recover for personal injuries received in a fall while attending an extracurricular event in the school. She was an invitee attending a baton twirling contest for the selection of majorettes in which her daughter was participating. She charged negligence against the board of education because her fall was allegedly caused by unsafe quantities of oil and wax on the floor. It was her contention that the board of education was liable in this case because the band and majorettes participated at football games—proprietary activities, and that the preliminary contest for the selection of majorettes was in the same category as a football game for which a fee was charged.

The question for the court to answer was: Is an athletic contest or any related activity conducted on school premises for monetary gain a proprietary or governmental function? The court held that the activities engaged in by the school did not constitute a proprietary function:

> . . . [I]t is the opinion of this court that the only monetary gain sought is the self-perpetuation of the activity engaged in by the student body, namely, football; therefore, it could not fall into the class of a profit-making enterprise. . . . [T]he attempt to make an athletic contest or any related activity thereto a proprietary function

---

16 Thompson ·v. Board of Ed. of Millville, 12 NJSuper 92, 79 A(2d) 100 (1951).

fails. The school building where the alleged accident took place was erected for the purpose of providing instruction for the children. . . . This is a definite governmental function, and the inclusion of the idea that football games are operated as a profit-making enterprise does not establish a transition from a governmental to a proprietary function.

It was the opinion of the court that since the organization of school athletic teams is generally considered a part of physical education, the school district is usually immune from liability for injuries, in the absence of wrongdoing, even though the holding of such is merely authorized and not mandatory.

A Pennsylvania court, disagreeing with the decision rendered by another Pennsylvania court in the Hoffman case,[17] said that a school district was not liable for injuries suffered by an athlete during a football game because the actual game, separate from its presentation to the public for an admission charge, was a governmental function.[18]

The plaintiff, whose injuries allegedly resulted from the use of defective football equipment, argued that the theory of the *Hoffman* case—liability for injuries sustained in connection with proprietary activities—should be extended to the player-participants in such a game, as well as to spectators who pay admission. The school district claimed immunity on the ground that (1) the conducting of and educational activity was a governmental function and (2) that the player in voluntarily participating in the game accepted the risks of injury involved therein.

The question that the court formulated for itself to answer was: "Should the character of the contest itself be changed from a classification within the field of governmental activities to one of proprietary activities simply because it is presented as a public spectacle for which spectators are charged admission?" Concluding that the contest itself was a governmental activity, as distinguished from the presentation of the

---

17 Hoffman v. Scranton School Dist., 67 D&C 301 (Pa, 1949).
18 Martini v. Olyphant Borough Sch. Dist., 83 D&C 206 (Pa, 1952).

contest on a commercial basis as a proprietary one, the court said:

> It is a matter of public knowledge that a good many undesirable features seem to have attached to the conduct of interscholastic, as well as inter-collegiate athletic contests. Nevertheless, such contests in themselves we think are clearly within the field of legitimate educational activities; they offer a controlled outlet to the unbounded energy and activity of youth as developed and encouraged in a program of physical education. They are desirable from the standpoint of encouraging within student bodies a widespread interest in such education and serve as proper tests of accomplishment in a particular educational field. So far as the players themselves are concerned, their coaches, managers, attendants and those engaged in providing the necessary facilities for the playing of the game, the field of educational and therefore governmental activity is broad enough to include them within its boundaries. We, therefore, distinguish the contest itself as an educational activity from the presentation of it to spectators on a commercial basis as a proprietary activity. On this theory there can be no liability on the school district employees to provide to the player the adequate and customary equipment which a player ought to have to protect himself against forseeable injury.

Deciding in favor of a defendant board of education, the Supreme Court of Michigan ruled that the plaintiff, a spectator who was injured when a section of bleachers collapsed, could not recover damages because the school district was performing a governmental function by providing for a program of interscholastic athletics.[19] The majority of the court concluded that the school board was ". . . performing a governmental function vested in it by law" when it sponsored athletic competition with other schools for which gate receipts were collected.

In disagreement with the majority of the court, Justice

---

[19] Richards v. School Dist. of Birminghan, 348 Mich 490, 83 NW(2d) 643 (1957).

Edwards, with whom Justice Smith concurred, wrote in the dissenting opinion:

> We . . . hold that defendant school district was . . . engaging in a "proprietary function" in the sponsoring of an athletic contest for which admission was charged, and hence cannot escape liability for negligent acts performed in relation to said contest on ground of governmental immunity.

The courts have not established any sound legal principle that can be applied universally to situations involving the distinction between governmental and proprietary functions. Some authorities recommend the elimination of the distinction between these two activities as an improvement to the American legal system:

> [M]uch loose thinking and loose use of the terms "governmental" and "proprietary" in legal decisions where they do not belong can be avoided. Legislation should be utilized to do away with the difference and to make the law in this field cease to be archaic, an instrument of injustice and a subject of criticism.[20]

Fuller and Casner also suggest ". . . that the present hit-or-miss application of partial tort liability be immediately replaced with a rule of complete tort liability."[21]

§ 6.3 Legal liability for injuries sustained in extracurricular activities in the absence of the proprietary-governmental question

Because of the tremendous number of cases dealing with tort liability of school personnel involved in the extracurricular activities program, an extensive study of all the available cases is not attempted. Only those cases which illustrate significant points, other than the proprietary-governmental question in relation to governmental immunity,

---

[20] Murray Seasongood, "Municipal Corporations: Objections to the Governmental or Proprietary Test," Virginia Law Review, XXII (June, 1936), p. 942.

[21] Edgar Fuller and A. James Casner, "Municipal Tort Liability in Operation," Harvard Law Review, LIV (January, 1941), p. 461.

are discussed in this section. For a thorough treatment of the field of general tort liability of school districts and tort liability in relation to the interscholastic athletic program, the reader is referred to the works of Martin[22] and Cleetwood,[23] respectively.

In some states there are statutory provisions which impose either complete or partial liability upon school districts. Washington is the only state in which a statute, because of its construction, has received the close scrutiny of the courts in deciding tort liability cases involving extracurricular activities. Protection for school districts from tort suits in connection with the public school athletic program is provided by statute in this state. Unlike the state of Washington, the legislatures of other states which have enacted laws holding a school district liable for its torts did not place limitations on various extracurricular activities. And the vast majority of the states have no statutory provisions abolishing immunity from torts at all.

Liability under specific statutes. Since Washington is the only state which makes specific statutory mention of extracurricular activities in regard to immunity from tort liability, all the litigation discussed in this subsection occurred in that state. Only those cases which involve the court's interpretation of the statute are herein discussed.

The law which the courts of Washington must interpret when deciding tort cases reads as follows:

> No action shall be brought or maintained against any school district or its officers for any noncontractual acts or omissions of such district, its agents, officers or employees, relating to any park, playground, or field house, athletic apparatus or appliance, or manual training equipment, whether situated in or about any schoolhouse or elsewhere, owned, operated or maintained by such school district.[24]

---

[22] David V. Martin, "Trends in Tort Liability of School Districts as Revealed by Court Decisions," Unpublished Ed. D. Dissertation, Duke University, 1962.

[23] Cleet C. Cleetwood, "Legal Liability for Injuries Sustained in a Public School Program of Interscholastic Athletics," Unpublished Ed. D. Dissertation, Duke University, 1959.

[24] Revised Code of Washington, Vol. 3, § 28.58.030.

The greatest problem that the courts of Washington have had in interpreting this statute is deciding on exactly what is meant by athletic "apparatus or appliance." The first case involving extracurricular activities in which the problem was dealt with occurred in 1934.[25] Action was brought against a school district by the guardian of a boy who was injured, by falling to the ground, when the guard rail on the back of the bleacher seats and upon which he was seated collapsed. The student, aware that the guard rail was not intended as a seat, occupied the position along with other spectators who were unable to find seats in the stands.

Deciding that the school board had the power to erect such seating facilities, the court had to determine whether the bleachers could be classified as an athletic apparatus or appliance within the meaning of the statute. Concluding that the bleachers did not come within this classification the court said:

> It is plain that the bleacher seats do not fall within the terms "athletic apparatus" or "manual training equipment," and we do not understand it to be contended otherwise. The question then is whether the bleacher seats were an appliance, and we are of the view they were not. Athletic apparatus, appliances, and manual training equipment are all things pertaining to the activities of those engaged in physical training or exercise, and they can have no reference to seats provided for mere spectators who assemble to view the activities upon the athletic field.

Although the bleachers were not considered to come within the category of an athletic apparatus or appliance, the plaintiff was unable to recover damages because the supreme court, in a second action, ruled that the boy was guilty of contributory negligence by sitting on a rail of which he was aware was not to be used as a seat.

In 1949, the same court ruled that a football was not an athletic apparatus or appliance, and that a school district could be held liable for injuries sustained in a game in which

---

[25] Juntila v. Everett Sch. Dist. No. 24, 178 Wash 637, 35 P(2d) 78 (1934); 183 Wash 357, 48 P(2d) 613 (1935) (second action).

a football was used and for which proper supervision was not provided.[26]

The plaintiff, a student who was injured while participating in an athletic game similar to football with fellow students on the school ground, brought action against the school board for being negligent in not providing proper supervision of the activity. From the trial court decision dismissing the action, the plaintiff appealed to the Supreme Court of Washington which reversed the decision and remanded the cause to the lower court with instructions for a new trial. The supreme court reasoned that a football was not an athletic apparatus or appliance in the following terms:

> In making a determination of this question, we note, first, that in a broad, general sense, a football might be considered to be an athletic apparatus or appliance. When, however, the relation of the words used, as to each other, and the text of the statute as a whole are carefully studied, we think that . . . the legislature intended by the words "athletic apparatus or appliance" . . . some sort of more or less permanently located equipment, such as swings, slides, traveling rings, teeter boards, chinning bars, etc., and not something as highly mobile as a football.

The court, therefore, restricted the meaning of athletic apparatus or appliance to permanently situated equipment or facilities and not to a highly mobile item such as a football. This interpretation is somewhat different from that given in *Juntila* v. *Everett School District*,[27] in which the court defined athletic apparatus and appliances as ". . . all things pertaining to the activities of those engaged in physical training and exercise."

In a 1951 case the Supreme Court of Washington ruled that a ". . . baseball backstop . . . [was] a playground athletic apparatus or appliance within the meaning of . . . [the statute]."[28] It was the contention of this court that "[t]he

---

[26] Briscoe v. School Dist. No. 123, Grays Harbor County, 32 Wash(2d) 352, 201 P(2d) 697 (1949).

[27] Juntila v. Everett Sch. Dist. No. 24, 178 Wash 637, 35 P(2d) 78 (1934); 183 Wash 357, 48 P(2d) 613 (1935) (second action).

[28] Snowden v. Kittitas County Sch. Dist. No. 401, 38 Wash(2d) 691, 231

word appliance is very broad and includes anything applied or used as a means to an end."

More recently the same court has followed the reasoning presented in the *Briscoe* case [29] by holding that a baseball was not an athletic apparatus or appliance. [30]

Action in this case was brought to recover damages for personal injuries suffered by a spectator at a high school baseball game held at the Hiawatha playfield, a public facility owned by the city of Seattle. The plaintiff, while attending an admission-free game, was hit on the left side of the face by a baseball thrown by one of the high school athletes who was "warming up." The impact of the baseball broke the plaintiff's full-plate denture at three places and cut and injured his face. In this suit the plaintiff alleged that the school district acted negligently by failing to provide adequate supervision of the baseball players.

The trial court dismissed the case by basing its decision on the immunity for acts ". . . relating to any park, playground, or field house, athletic apparatus or appliance. . . ." Failing to receive a favorable judgment from the trial court, the plaintiff appealed the case to the Supreme Court of Washington. This court, supporting the thesis presented in the *Briscoe* case, declined to declare a baseball, a highly mobile object, an athletic apparatus or appliance. Although the decision was reversed and remanded to the trial court by a majority of the supreme court, three justices dissented. Supporting the opinion of the court in the *Snowden* case, [31] in which the word "appliance" was given the broad meaning to include ". . . anything applied or used as a means to an end," Chief Justice Ott in the dissenting opinion said:

> I find nothing in the immunity statute that includes a legislative intent that the words and phrases "relating to," "playground," "athletic apparatus or appliance," "owned,

---

P(2d) 621 (1951).

   [29] Briscoe v. School Dist. No. 123, Grays Harbor County, 32 Wash(2d) 352, 201 P(2d) 697 (1949).

   [30] Barnecut v. Seattle Sch. Dist. No. 1, 63 Wash(2d) 905, 389 P(2d) 904 (1964).

   [31] Snowden v. Kittitas County Sch. Dist. No. 401, 38 Wash(2d) 691, 231 P(2d) 621 (1951).

operated, or maintained," should be given a limited or restricted meaning.

A spectator watching a free baseball game on a school playground has no cause of action against the school district, when he is hit by a baseball while sitting in the bleachers, because the district, by statute, owes such a person no duty of care.

A baseball is an appliance because this court . . . said in the Snowden case that "The word "appliance" is very broad and includes anything applied or used as a means to an end." More than 12 years later, a majority of this court now reversed the Snowden case and say that a baseball is not an appliance "used as a means to an end" in the game of baseball. Should this interpretation gain nationwide acceptance, we could be watching the World Series in pantomime.

In another case involving extracurricular activities the Supreme Court of Washington awarded damages to the parents of a boy who was fatally injured during an initiation into a school athletic letter society.[32] The tragedy occurred on a school day and while the student was under the care of the school district's agents. The court held the school district liable for negligence:

By statute, the liability of the school district for negligence is the same as the liability of any person or corporation except that a school district has absolute immunity for accidents resulting from "any athletic apparatus or appliance or manual training equipment." This action is not within the exception.

The problem of exactly what the Washington legislature meant by athletic "apparatus or appliance" is not satisfactorily resolved, but several decisions, including the most recent one, appear to follow the line of reasoning that a mobile object, such as a ball, is not an athletic apparatus or appliance, but that a permanent, nonmobile object used in

---

32 Sherwood v. Moxee Sch. Dist. No.90, 363 P(2d) 138 (Wash, 1961).

games, such as a baseball backstop or some similar object, is an athletic apparatus or appliance for which a school district can be held liable for accidents resulting therefrom.

Liability in the absence of specific statutes. Since none of the states other than Washington have legislation which specifically mentions extracurricular activities in regard to immunity from tort liability, most litigation falls within this category.

A teacher is a governmental employee and is not immune from personal liability for acts of negligence while performing his duties.[33] While supervising extracurricular activities, particularly athletics, a teacher must use a reasonable degree of care. "Failure to furnish adequate supervision which causes injuries is an act for which a teacher is liable,[34] and "[l]ack of supervision of pupils or improper supervision may constitute negligence on the part of the school district."[35]

The law requires that a teacher, while in charge of pupils, exercise the care of a reasonably prudent person. Extracurricular advisors, athletic coaches in particular, can be found guilty of negligence for not conducting themselves as reasonably prudent persons.

This standard does not make teachers the insurers of the safety of children. If school personnel have acted as the reasonable, prudent parent under the circumstance and nevertheless a child is injured, the teacher or administrator cannot be held responsible. The teacher and administrator are not liable for pure accidents.[36]

Injuries sustained by participants. The Supreme Court of the state of Washington—a state in which the legislature has abolished school district immunity from tort liability in cer-

---

33 Edwards, The Courts and the Public Schools, p. 474.
34 Hamilton and Mort, The Law and Public Education, p. 292.
35 Woodsmall v. Mt. Diablo Unified Sch. Dist., 10 CalRptr 447 (1961).
36 Reynolds C. Seitz, "Legal Responsibility Under Tort Law of School Personnel and School Districts as Regards Negligent Conduct Toward Pupils," Hasting Law Journal, XV (May, 1964), pp. 496-97.

tain situations—held that a school district was liable for the negligent acts of a football coach.[37]

A high school athletic coach persuaded and coerced a seventeen-year-old boy into practicing as a member of the football team. The boy injured his back and spine during practice and then two weeks later, while still suffering from the injury, the coach required him to play on the football team. During the course of the game the athlete, in addition to internal injuries, suffered further serious injuries to his back and spine.

The father of the injured boy brought action to recover medical expenses and loss of services of his minor son as a result of the negligence of the athletic coach. The court, rendering a decision favorable to the plaintiff, pointed out that it repeatedly held that a school district is liable for negligent acts of its officers and agents acting within the scope of their authority:

> [I] f the school district organized and maintained a football team and one of its teachers, with the knowledge and consent of the board of directors, acted as coach and trainer thereof, and if the coach knew that a student in the school was physically unable to play football, or in the exercise of reasonable care should have known it, but nevertheless permitted, persuaded and coerced such student to play, with the result that he sustained injuries, the district would be liable.

A California court also awarded damages to a high school athlete who sustained severe and permanent injury as a result of the negligence of a football coach.[38]

The plaintiff, a member of the high school football team, was injured when he was tackled during a football scrimmage. After being tackled he was lying on his back and unable to get to his feet. Suspecting that the boy might have a neck injury, the coach had him hold out his hands to see if there was any grip in them. At this time the plaintiff was able to

---

[37] Morris v. Union High Sch. Dist. A, King County, 160 Wash 121, 294 Pac 998 (1931).

[38] Welch v. Dunsmuir Joint Union High Sch. Dist., 326 P(2d) 633 (Cal, 1958).

move his hands. Although there was conflicting testimony as to whether a doctor was present at the time of the accident, the injured boy was then definitely removed from the football field by eight boys, four on each side, without the aid of a stretcher and without any directions from anyone. After being removed from the field, the plaintiff was unable to move his hands, fingers, and feet.

At the trial, the doctor who testified about the medical condition of the plaintiff said that since the boy could move his hands before but not after being moved from the field, additional injury was sustained by moving him without the use of a stretcher. The doctor testified that the plaintiff suffered damage to the spinal cord at the level of the fifth cervical vertebra, which resulted in permanent paralysis of all four limbs.

The school district appealed the case to the district court of appeal, after receiving an adverse judgment from the trial court jury. The defendants contended that the lower court erred and was prejudicial by giving the jury an instruction in the following language: "Because of the great danger involved in moving an injured human being a person of ordinary prudence will exercise extreme caution when engaged in such an activity. Hence it is the duty of anyone managing or participating in such an activity to exercise extreme caution." Finding no merit in the defendant's objection, the court ruled that the school district was obliged to pay damages to the plaintiff.

A case recently came before the Supreme Court of Oregon in which negligence was charged on the ground that a high school student was injured as a result of his being an "inexperienced football player."[39] In a judgment favorable to the school district the court ruled that the football coach was not negligent in directing this boy to play football, on the theory that a participant in a lawful game assumes the dangers inherent therein.

The appellate division of the superior court of New Jersey did not hold athletic coaches liable for failing to obtain

---

[39] Vendrell v. School Dist. No. 26C, Malheur County, 226 Ore 263, 360 P(2d) 282 (1961); 233 Ore 1, 376 P(2d) 406 (1962).

immediate medical attention for a football player who was not seriously injured.[40]

While participating in football practice, the plaintiff dislocated his shoulder in an attempt to recover a fumble. The coach put the boy's arm in a sling after "snapping it back in place." On the following day the coach sent the plaintiff to the school physician, who examined his shoulder and told him that he would be able to return to football practice in two weeks.

Two weeks later the boy informed the coach that he could return to practice with the football team. Under the direction of another coach for tackle practice, the plaintiff again dislocated his shoulder the first time he tackled another player. He could not get up, and when the coach assisted him his shoulder snapped in place by itself. The boy then returned to the clubhouse where he was informed by the other coach that he was to return his equipment, as he would not be able to play football for the remainder of the year. Upon asking the coach, the boy was informed that he did not have to return to the school physician this time. After the coach put his arm in a sling, the plaintiff walked home with another boy who carried his books. For three days thereafter he wore the sling in the presence of his parents and was not absent from school.

When the boy brought action against the coaches for alleged negligence in failing to obtain medical attention during an emergency which allegedly existed when he was accidentally injured during football practice, the court concluded that there was insufficient evidence to make out a case for a jury:

> It is clear that this evidence and the inferences which may legitimately be drawn therefrom in no wise could support a finding of an immediate pressing necessity for medical aid for the boy before he went home and that the decision whether to obtain such aid could not await his parent's consideration. He was fully possessed of his faculties, was able to walk unattended the 125 yards from the

---

[40] Duda v. Gaines, 12 NJSuper 326, 79 A(2d) 695 (1951).

field to the clubhouse and after changing clothes to walk home. In these circumstances the facts do not reasonably permit opposing conclusions by far-minded men as to whether or not the boy was then in urgent need of medical attention.

The need for a teacher to be a reasonably careful and prudent person is illustrated by an incident in which an athlete was killed by an electrical shock received at the hands of fellow pupils and a coach during an athletic club initiation.[41]

A high school letter club planned an initiation ceremony for which the athletic coach obtained the permission of the superintendent of schools to use the high school gymnasium. The members of the club constructed a device for administering an electrical shock to the initiates by using an electrical outlet in the school building as the source of electricity instead of a battery which was customarily used. The apparatus consisted of a crude rheostat made from a jar of distilled water in which a quantity of salt was dissolved. Several wires were placed on the gymnasium floor and each initiate had to assume a prostrate position across the wires while balancing a container of water on his chest. When the shock was administered the initiate would jump and the container of water would spill over him and the floor. The fourth boy subjected to this ordeal, on a wet floor, complained of a great shock. One of the members of the club then replaced some of the salt water in the jar with tap water, and the group proceeded with the activities. The next boy to receive the shock was electrocuted and died almost instantly.

At the ensuing trial the jury found both the superintendent of schools and the athletic coach guilty of negligence. The school district then appealed the case to the Supreme Court of South Dakota.

The coach contended that he had no official jurisdication or supervision over the club members during the initiation. But since he gave the boys permission to use the electrical device, tested its wires, and was in full charge of the club, the

---

[41] DeGooyer v. Harkness, 70 SD 26, 13 NW(2d) 815 (1944).

court concluded that he was liable whether or not he was acting in his official capacity as coach.

> The facts disclose . . . [the coach] actively participated in the initiation activities, that it was he who tested the electrical appliance, and that he played an active role in this whole procedure of administering the electrical shock. We are of the opinion therefore, that so far as his liability is concerned it is immaterial whether he was acting in a personal capacity or in his capacity as athletic coach or teacher.

Although the court sustained the jury's decision regarding the coach, it failed to hold the superintendent of schools liable for the negligence of the athletic coach because the coach agreed, when obtaining permission to use the gymnasium, that he would be present to supervise the activities.

Deciding a case in which a school district was allegedly negligent for not providing supervision of a club initiation ceremony, the Supreme Court of Washington ruled in favor of the defendant board of education. [42]

A student brought suit against a school district to recover damages for an injury sustained in an automobile accident which occurred as he and another pupil returned home from a club initiation. The ceremony, at which alcoholic beverages were served, was not supervised by school personnel. It was alleged that the school district had approved an advisor to assist and supervise the club, but that no check was kept on club activities. The court ruled in favor of the school district by saying that there was no cause for action against it for the accident which occurred at 2:00 a.m. on a Sunday morning. The court said that " . . . the negligence charged . . . [was] failure to supervise, . . . [but that] the events which resulted in the injuries to the plaintiff could not have been anticipated as arising from the breach of duty."

In a more recent case, the Supreme Court of New York found two teachers, charged with the responsibility of conducting a softball championship game, negligent for failing to provide adequate supervision of spectators whose close

---

[42] Coates v. Tacoma Sch. Dist. No. 10, 347 P(2d) 1093 (Wash, 1960).

proximity to the baseball diamond was responsible for an injury to a player.[43]

Along the periphery of the baseball diamond, between home plate and first and third bases, were situated benches for the use of the competing teams. These benches were placed against a fence which surrounded that portion of the baseball diamond. During the course of the game the benches were appropriated by spectators who moved them forward toward the foul line. Spectators also occupied the space in front of the benches. Twice during the contest the game had to be stopped by the supervising teachers in order to move the fans back to the fence, but each time the spectators gradually moved forward again. When a foul ball was hit into the crowd between home plate and third base the catcher, looking up while pursuing the ball, tripped over a spectator, fell over the bench, and broke his leg.

Action was taken against the two teachers who were supervising the game for alleged negligence for failing to supervise adequately and restrain the spectators. At the trial, the court informed the jury that a board of education acts as a legal individual and is liable for the negligence of its officers in charge of playgrounds and facilities:

> [I] n maintaining playgrounds, the City or any of its agencies, and that includes the Board of Education, . . . acts as a legal individual and is not immune from liability for the negligence of its officers given charge and authority over such playgrounds and the apparatus there contained.

The board of education argued that the charge was erroneous, since it authorized the jury to find it liable under the principle of *respondeat superior* and made it liable for negligence of its personnel without itself being guilty of negligence in the selection of its teachers and personnel.

The supreme court, overruling the objection of the board of education, agreed with the decision of the jury that there was sufficient evidence to support the plaintiff's charge of negligence, because both teachers were present at the game and the gradual movement of the spectators was obvious. The

---

[43] Domino v. Mercurio, 234 NYS(2d) 1011 (1962).

court also ruled that the plaintiff was not guilty of contributory negligence and was not chargeable with a voluntary assumption of a known risk in connection with his injury. Reaffirming the fact that the state of New York became liable for the negligence of its teachers under the Court of Claims Act of 1929, the majority of the court said:

> We have come to the conclusion that the charge was correct and that the Board [of Education] was properly held liable in this case. In our opinion, the charge represents the present law, although no appellate court has as yet spelled out the liability of Boards of Education in as broad terms as those used by the trial court in this case.

While supporting the principle of liability of a board of education for the negligent acts of its teachers, two justices dissented on the ground that there was insufficient evidence to prove the teachers negligent. Justices Williams and Henry expressed their opinion as follows:

> We dissent and vote to reverse the judgment and grant a new trial. While we agree with the general principle of liability of a Board of Education for the negligence of its teachers stated in the prevailing opinion, we fail to find any evidence in this case that the defendant teachers were negligent. . . . On this record it cannot be found that the accident resulted from any lack of proper supervision by the defendants. . . . Adequate supervision would not have prevented the accident.

In another case decided during the same year, the Supreme Court of New York refused to hold a board of education liable for the alleged negligent act of a head coach which resulted in the injury of an assistant coach during baseball practice.[44]

At a practice session the head coach, situated at home plate, would bunt balls along the base lines or toward the pitcher. A player would then run toward first base and the infielders and the pitcher would try to put the runner "out." The plaintiff, an assistant coach, was located behind the

---

[44] McGee v. Board of Ed. of New York, 226 NYS(2d) 329 (1962).

pitcher's box for the purpose of giving the pitcher directions. During one play a runner left second base and proceeded toward third base, and the head coach shouted "Get the man at third" to the first baseman. The first baseman, responding to the order, threw the ball toward third base and hit the assistant coach who was directly between first and third bases.

The coach brought action against the school board to recover damages on the theory that the head coach acted negligently in laying out a nonregulation practice field, on which the pitcher's mound was situated directly between first and third bases, and by directing the first baseman to throw the ball to third base.

The supreme court of New York County rendered a decision favorable to the teacher, but when the board of education appealed the case, the Supreme Court of New York State reversed the decision. The court said:

> Generally the participants in an athletic event are held to have assumed the risks of injury normally associated with the sport. Players, coaches, managers, referees and others who, in one way or another, voluntarily participate must accept the risks to which these rules expose them. Of course, this is not to say that actionable negligence can never be committed on a playing field. Considering the skill of the players, the rules and nature of the particular game, and risks which normally attend it, a participant's conduct may amount to such careless disregard for the safety of others as to create risks not fairly assumed. But it is nevertheless true that what the scorekeeper may record as an "error" is not the equivalent, in law, of negligence.

. . . .

> The head coach and the players could reasonably expect that plaintiff, an experienced player, would be alert to the dangers. Thus, when the call was shouted to "Get the man at third," neither the head coach nor the first baseman would have had any occasion to warn plaintiff, or anyone else, to watch out for the throw. The athlete's maxim, "keep your eye on the ball," was just as applicable in this situation as in a regular game.

Deciding a tort liability case which was brought as a result of a transportation accident, a United States district court upheld an Oklahoma school district's claim that it was not liable for injuries sustained by persons who were involved in an accident with a school bus which the board of education had provided to transport students on a senior class trip. [45]

The school district authorized the use of a school bus to transport the members of the senior class of Turpin High School to the auto races at Indianapolis, Indiana. Two adults, Maynard Smith, the bus driver, and Betty Smith, served as chaperones for the trip. Three members of the board of education were participants in the activity, but the evidence does not clearly indicate whether they were passengers on the bus.

While enroute to Indiana the bus was involved in an accident in Kansas with two other vehicles—one from Kansas and one from Arizona. The plaintiffs, all members of the automobile from Arizona, brought action against the board of education and the passengers of the bus to recover damages for personal injuries. The three members of the board of education involved in the activity, the chaperones, and the students were all named in the suit because, according to the plaintiffs, they were participants in a joint venture and the alleged negligence of the driver applied to them all. The plaintiffs charged the board of education with negligence because it (1) authorized and participated in an out-of-state excursion which was in violation of Oklahoma statutes; (2) permitted the use of a dilapidated bus with defective brakes to be used for such a trip; (3) and allowed Smith, an allegedly reckless driver who had faulty vision, to drive the bus.

The defendants moved to dismiss the case because they contended that the school district, a governmental subdivision of Oklahoma, was acting in a public or governmental capacity by providing free transportation for the senior class excursion. They also pointed out that if the providing of transportation for an out-of-state trip was illegal as the plain-

---

[45] Thurman v. Consolidated Sch. Dist. No. 128, Turpin, 94 FSupp 616 (Okla, 1950).

tiffs alleged, then the act was *ultra vires* for which there was
no legal liability.

Although thc plaintiffs charged that the defendants could
not rely on the defense of *ultra vires* to defeat the ends of
justice, the court did not agree:

> It would be anomalous, to say the least, if a school
> district which cannot be required to respond in damages
> when legally transporting its children to school, could be
> subjected to such damages because its board permitted
> such bus to be used in an illegal out-of-state excursion.

It is possible that teachers might be held personally liable
for injuries to students resulting from transportation accidents if arrangements for such transportation are made by
the teachers without official approval of the school board.
The Supreme Court of Wisconsin found a school district not
liable for injuries sustained by a pupil of another school district who was invited by two coaches, without the approval
or knowledge of the board of education, to travel to an extracurricular event on one of the school district's buses.[46]

The school bus was owned by the city of Eau Claire,
Wisconsin, and at the invitation of the debating coaches, students from a nearby school district were transported to a
debating contest along with the Eau Claire team. Suit was
filed by one of thc invitees who was injured in an accident.

It was the opinion of the court that the school district
could not be held liable for the injury to the pupil in this case
because the teachers had no authority to invite him to travel
on the Eau Claire bus without the consent of the board of
education:

> [T]hese coaches had no more authority, without
> authorization by the school board, than the driver, to
> invite the . . . .[neighboring] team aboard. They could
> no more authorize the taking of the . . . team than any
> ordinary fellow servant of the driver of a truck could with-
> out authorization from the master, impose liability on the
> master for negligence of the driver by telling the driver to
> permit a person to ride with him.

---

[46] Huettner v. Eau Claire, 243 Wis 80, 9 NW(2d) 583 (1943).

In an Idaho case, a teacher who permitted her automobile to be used by an athletic coach to transport players to a football game was held personally liable for the injuries sustained by a student when the automobile was involved in an accident.[47]

A football coach borrowed another teacher's automobile to transport several of his players to a football game. The accident, in which the coach was killed and one of the players was severely injured, occurred on the way to the game. In awarding damages to the plaintiffs, the injured boy and his parents, the Supreme Court of Idaho ruled that the deceased coach had acted as the agent of the teacher owning the automobile and that she was liable for the injury sustained by the boy as a result of the accident.

As these representative cases indicate, a teacher who does not exercise the care of a reasonably prudent person might be held liable for negligent acts conducted by him during the course of his scope of employment. In states other than those in which governmental immunity has been abrogated or in which "save harmless" laws exist, a teacher could be held personally liable for his negligence because the injured person could not recover from the board of education unless the court decided that the act of negligence occurred during an activity which was proprietary in nature and for which the school district could not claim governmental immunity. This problem was dealt with in a previous section of this chapter.

Injuries sustained by spectators. It is not uncommon for a spectator to be injured while witnessing an athletic contest. As was illustrated by the cases discussed in an earlier section of this chapter, injured spectators frequently bring action against the school district on the ground that the activity for which they paid admission to attend was a proprietary enterprise and that the school district by sponsoring such an event had waived its governmental immunity. Only those cases which do not involve the question of governmental immunity in relation to governmental and proprietary activities are discussed in this subsection.

---

[47] Gorton v. Doty, 69 P(2d) 136 (Idaho, 1937).

An action in tort for damages resulting from injuries sustained by a spectator while an invitee at a public school field day exhibition was taken against the members of a board of education in Indiana.[48] The plaintiff, a spectator at a school event for which she paid admission, was seriously injured when faulty temporary seats upon which she was seated collapsed and threw her to the ground. Action was taken against all of the members and the clerk of the board of education individually. The board of education had nothing to do with the activity except to authorize the clerk to have the temporary seats constructed. From a judgment for the defendants, the plaintiff appealed the case to the appellate court of Indiana.

The question in this case involved the distinction between discretionary and ministerial acts and the liability for negligence therewith attached. Affirming the discretionary right of a school board to make all the necessary arrangements for the field day exercises which relate to the physical education and athletic development of the pupils, the court held that the board of education could not be held liable for any negligence as a result of such acts:

> A duty is discretionary when it involves on the part of the officer to determine whether or not he should perform a certain act, and, if so, in what particular way, and in the absence of corrupt motives in the exercise of such discretion he is not liable. His duties, however, in the performance of the act, after he has once determined that it shall be done, are ministerial, and for negligence in such performance, which results in injury, he may be liable for damages.

By reversing its judgment, the appellate court instructed the trial court to grant a new trial. Describing the condition under which the board of education could be held liable, the court said:

> [W]e hold that the appellees, members of the school board, in determining that there should be field day exer-

---

[48] Adams v. Schneider, 71 IndApp 249, 124 NE 718 (1919).

cises, in connection with their school, were acting within their jurisdiction, and that such act, together with their action in determining the manner in which such exercises should be conducted was discretionary, and that for injuries resulting therefrom they are not liable, but that the duties performed in making preparation for such field day exercises and the general management thereof were ministerial acts, for the negligent performance of which, if so performed, whether performed by themselves, by their agents, or by an independent contractor, they were liable for damages for injuries suffered by reason thereof. It follows that the duties performed by the appellee clerk of the board were ministerial acts, and for their negligent performance, if so performed, he was jointly liable with his coappellees.

It was also pointed out by the court that a school district, like any owner of a public place, should exercise care in seeing that its facilities are safe for public use.

Those who accept the invitation to attend and who have paid the admission fee have a right to assume that a safe place has been prepared for them, and it is not to be expected of them that they make an inspection of the surroundings for the purpose of determining whether or not they are safe.

A complaint alleging negligence was brought against a California school district to recover for injuries sustained by a student spectator at a football game when she was struck by a bottle thrown by a fellow student.[49] The plaintiff, along with numerous other students, attended a football game held in the California Memorial Stadium at Berkeley, sponsored by the school district which had teachers present to supervise the students. Some pupils seated above the plaintiff engaged in rowdyism by throwing objects on the spectators below, and in the course of their disorderly conduct the plaintiff was injured by a heavy glass bottle which was thrown by one of the disorderly pupils.

---

[49] Weldy v. Oakland High School of Alameda County, 19 CalApp(2d) 429, 65 P(2d) 851 (1937).

It was the contention of the plaintiff that the school district was negligent because no attempt was made to remedy the dangerous situation by subduing the unruly pupils. The court pointed out that the liability of a school district for injuries to its students, as authorized by statute, does not permit recovery unless the injuries arise from the negligence of the district or its personnel: "The statute does not create a liability upon the district for injuries arising from the unlawful or willful misconduct of its students." The only way a school district could be held liable for injuries so inflicted would be to prove that it was guilty of some act of commission or omission amounting to negligence. Elaborating on this point the court said:

[I]f experience had demonstrated that a game of football was likely to be attended by rowdyism and injury to spectators the school district might be held bound to anticipate "such consequences as a reasonably prudent man would anticipate as likely to result therefrom." . . . But we cannot say as a matter of law that rowdyism is the natural attendant of a game of football or that the district should have foreseen that such would be the result of this particular game. The complaint does not allege that the district, or any of its employees, had knowledge of the alleged rowdyism, nor that these employees failed to do any act which failure was negligent on their part. The general allegation that the district negligently and carelessly failed to exercise supervision over the conduct of the students is unavailing when no facts are alleged upon which the conclusion of negligence is based.

A similar conclusion was reached by the court in an earlier case dealing with the injury of a student by falling theatrical scenery as a result of the negligence of fellow students. The court held that a school district could not be sued for injuries caused by the negligent acts of students. [50]
In another California case a school district was held liable

---

[50] Hack v. Sacramento City Jr. College Dist. of Sacramento, 21 P(2d) 477 (Calif, 1933).

for injuries suffered by a child, not a pupil of the school, who was injured while attending a baseball game.[51]

The child, who came to the baseball game with adults, was permitted to wander about the school campus and was severely cut by a sharp piece of glass which was located in an abandoned broadjumping pit in which she was playing. After receiving an adverse judgment from the trial court, the plaintiff appealed the case to the district court of appeal, which reversed the decision by saying that the "[d]efendants may be liable for negligence for failure to reasonably anticipate the use of such equipment by children."

When a spectator, after being injured by falling from an elevated area in a school parking lot, brought action against a school district for violation of a safe place statute, the Supreme Court of Wisconsin concluded that the school district had no duty to the plaintiff imposed by the safe place statute because of the construction and maintenance of the elevated area and ramp from which he fell.[52] The court was of the opinion that the plaintiff could have used the public walk to the gymnasium door instead of the entrance to the boiler room where the accident occurred.

§ 6.4   Summary

Because of the frequency of accidents involving both participants and spectators of interscholastic athletics, tort liability cases constitute the majority of the litigation involving the extracurricular program of public schools.

Since the rule of *respondeat superior* does not apply in most school tort cases, teachers can be held personally liable for their negligent acts. In the area of extracurricular activities it is the athletic coach who is most vulnerable as a result of governmental immunity, for accidents occur most frequently in interscholastic athletics, and a coach who is found negligent for the injury of an athlete can be compelled to pay damages to the student.

Although the courts and legislatures of some states have modified the doctrine of governmental immunity, the

---

[51] Brown v. Oakland, 51 CalApp(2d) 150, 124 P(2d) 369 (1942).
[52] Hemmingway v. Janesville, 275 Wis 304, 81 NW(2d) 492 (1957).

majority of the school districts in the United States are immune from liability. In states where governmental immunity prevails, the courts have permitted recovery in some cases if the injuries were sustained while the school district was performing proprietary functions.[53] Numerous plaintiffs have brought suit on the ground that the board of education was engaged in a private or proprietary activity for which it could not claim immunity from tort liability. This legal approach is particularly common in actions to recover damages for injuries sustained in connection with extra-curricular events, namely interscholastic athletic contests for which admission was charged.

The courts have been unable to agree on a precise distinction between governmental and proprietary functions; consequently, it is difficult to determine into which category a given activity will be placed until after a court has ruled. A Pennsylvania court declared that an athletic contest for which admission was charged was a proprietary activity which was outside the authority of the school district to perform.[54] The court, therefore, rendered a decision favorable to the plaintiff, who was injured while attending a football game. Similarly, the Supreme Court of Arizona ruled that a school district, by leasing its stadium, had engaged in a proprietary act and that it could be held liable for injuries sustained as a result of its negligence to maintain the stadium.[55] The Pennsylvania Supreme Court more recently declared that a school district which offered a summer recreation program, not part of the school curriculum and for which admission was charged, was conducting a proprietary activity and was therefore liable, because of negligence, for the death of a girl who drowned in the swimming pool.[56]

Not all courts have been willing to declare that a school district can be held liable for injuries resulting from negligent

[53] See Morris v. School Dist. of the Tp. of Mount Lebanon, 393 Pa 663, 144 A(2d) 737 (1958).

[54] Hoffman v. Scranton Sch. Dist., 67 D&C 301 (Pa, 1949).

[55] Sawaya v. Tucson High Sch. Dist. of Pima County, 78 Ariz 389, 281 P(2d) 105 (1955).

[56] Morris v. School Dist. of the Tp. of Mount Lebanon, 393 Pa 633, 144 A(2d) 737 (1958).

acts of its employees, when such acts are associated with an activity which might be classifed as proprietary. When a woman, injured by a baseball which came through a protective screen which had been negligently permitted to deteriorate, sought damages on the ground that the board of education was liable because the activity was a proprietary one, the district court of appeal of Florida failed to be persuaded by her argument, even though she cited the *Hoffman*[57] and *Sawaya*[58] cases in support of her claim.[59] The court asserted that any change in the immunity doctrine would have to come about by constitutional amendment or by the passage of appropriate legislation, or both.

The Supreme Courts of Minnesota[60] and Montana[61] upheld the doctrine of governmental immunity by ruling that the charge of admission did not change a school district's activity from a governmental to a proprietary classification. Other courts have ruled that interscholastic athletics are part of the physical education program and cannot be designated as proprietary activities,[62] and that a school district definitely performs a governmental function by providing for interscholastic athletics.[63]

There is, however, a difference of opinion among the courts of the various jurisdictions in regard to which activities are governmental and which are proprietary. A Tennessee court held that a school district, because of its legal status, could conduct itself in no other than a governmental capacity;[64] yet, a court in Pennsylvania ruled that while the actual athletic competition of interscholastic events was a

---

[57] Hoffman v. Scranton School Dist., 67 D&C 301 (Pa, 1949).
[58] Sawaya v. Tucson High Sch. Dist. of Pima County, 78 Ariz 389, 281 P(2d) 105 A(2d) 737 (1955).
[59] Buck v. McLean, 115 S(2d) 764 (Fla, 1959).
[60] Mokovich v. Independent Sch. Dist. of Va., No. 22, 177 Minn 446, 225 NW 292 (1929).
[61] Rhoades v. School Dist. No. 9, Roosevelt County, 115 Mont 352, 142 P(2d) 890 (1943).
[62] Watson v. School Dist. of Bay City, 324 Mich 1, 36 NW(2d) 195 (1949); Thompson v. Board of Ed., City of Millville, 12 NJSuper 92, 79 A(2d) 100 (1951).
[63] Richards v. School Dist. of Birmingham, 348 Mich 490, 83 NW(2d) 643 (1957).
[64] Reed v. Rhea County, 189 Tenn 247, 225 SW(2d) 49 (1949).

governmental activity, its presentation to the public for a charge was a proprietary enterprise.[65]

Although the consensus is not unanimous, the majority of the courts have ruled that the board of education does not operate outside of its governmental capacity by supporting enterprises which produce funds for the support of extra-curricular activities. Nevertheless, the courts have not established any sound legal principle that can be applied universally to situations involving the distinction between governmental and proprietary functions. Some authorities recommend the elimination of such a distinction and the establishment of complete tort liability as an improvement to the American legal system.

In tort liability cases in which the proprietary-governmental distinction is not a question, it remains for the plaintiff to prove negligence on the part of a school employee and, in some cases, to convince the court that his claim is a legitimate one under a state statute, particularly when the statute, such as the one which exists in Washington, places restrictions on recovery. The Washington law prohibits recovery for injuries sustained in relation " . . . to any park, playground, or field house, athletic apparatus or appliance. . . ."[66] The problem for the courts of the state of Washington has been the definition of the terms athletic "apparatus" and "appliance." In a 1934 case, the court ruled that bleacher seats did not come within the category of athletic apparatus or appliance, but recovery of damages was denied a spectator who was injured at an athletic event because of his contributory negligence.[67] In 1949, the same court declared that a football was not an athletic apparatus or appliance, and that a school district could be held liable for negligently failing to provide adequate supervision of a game in which a player was injured.[68] The court restricted the meaning of athletic "apparatus or appliance" to permanently

---

[65] Martini v. Olyphant Borough Sch. Dist., 83 D&C 206 (Pa, 1952).
[66] Revised Code of Washington, Vol. 3, § 28.58.030.
[67] Juntila v. Everett Sch. Dist. No. 24, 178 Wash 637, 35 P(2d) 78 (1934); 183 Wash 357, 48 P(2d) 613 (1935) (second action).
[68] Briscoe v. School Dist. No. 123, Grays Harbor County, 32 Wash(2d) 352, 201 P(2d) 697 (1949).

situated equipment. The Supreme Court of Washington, in a 1951 case, ruled that a baseball backstop was a playground athletic apparatus or appliance within the meaning of the statute; [69] it said that the meaning of these terms ". . . is very broad and includes anything applied or used as a means to an end." However, the same court more than a decade later, in 1964, concluded that a baseball was not an athletic apparatus or appliance, and that a school district could be held liable for injuries sustained by a spectator who was injured when he was struck by a baseball. [70] Although the problem of what the Washington legislature meant by athletic "apparatus or appliance" remains unresolved, several decisions, including the most recent one, appear to follow the line of reasoning that a mobile object, such as a ball, is not an athletic apparatus or appliance, but that a permanent, non-mobile object used in the game comes within the meaning of the terms.

A teacher, a governmental employee, is not immune from personal liability for acts of negligence while performing his duties, and his failure to supervise pupils adequately might constitute negligence on the part of the school district. Athletic coaches have been held liable for injuries resulting from coercing pupils to participate in athletic contests, [71] and for not exercising reasonable care when moving an injured athlete. [72] However, in other jurisdictions the courts have held that a coach was not negligent for permitting an allegedly "inexperienced football player" to participate in an interscholastic event, [73] or for failing to obtain immediate medical attention for a student who was not seriously injured. [74]

---

[69] Snowden v. Kittitas County Sch. Dist. No. 401, 38 Wash(2d) 961, 231 P(2d) 621 (1951).
[70] Barnecut v. Seattle Sch. Dist. No. 1, 63 Wash(2d) 905, 389 P(2d) 904 (1964).
[71] Morris v. Union High Sch. Dist. A, King County, 160 Wash 121, 294 Pac 998 (1931).
[72] Welch v. Dunsmuir Joint Union High Sch. Dist., 326 P(2d) 633 (Calif, 1958).
[73] Vendrell v. School Dist. No. 26C, Malheur County, 226 Ore 263, 360 P(2d) 282 (1961); 233 Ore 1, 376 P(2d) 406 (1962).
[74] Duda v. Gaines, 12 NJSuper 326, 79 A(2d) 695 (1951)

The need for a teacher to be a reasonably careful and prudent person is illustrated by an incident in which a high school student was accidently electrocuted at the hands of fellow pupils during an athletic club initiation.[75] Although the athletic coach contended that he had no official jurisdiction or supervision over the club members during the initiation, he was held liable for the accident because he gave the students permission to use an electrical shocking appliance, tested its wires, and was in full charge of the club at the time of the accident. In a similar case in which a school district was allegedly negligent for not providing supervision of a club initiation ceremony, the court ruled in favor of the defendant board of education.[76] The court held that there was no cause for action against the board of education for injuries suffered by a student in an automobile accident which occurred after a club initiation ceremony at 2:00 a.m. on a Sunday morning, for the events which resulted in the injuries to the plaintiff could not have been anticipated and did not arise from a breach of duty.

More recently, the Supreme Court of New York found two teachers, charged with the responsibility of conducting a softball game, negligent for failing to provide adequate supervision of spectators whose close proximity to the baseball diamond was responsible for an injury to a player.[77] In another New York case decided during the same year, the court refused to hold a board of education liable for the alleged negligent act of a head coach which resulted in the injury of an assistant coach during baseball practice.[78]

Deciding a tort liability case involving a transportation accident, a United States district court upheld an Oklahoma school district's claim that it was not liable for injuries sustained by persons who were involved in an accident with a school bus which the board of education had provided to transport students on a senior class trip.[79] Teachers might,

---

75 DeGooyer v. Harkness, 70 SD 26, 13 NW(2d) 815 (1944).
76 Coates v. Tacoma Sch. Dist. No. 10, 347 P(2d) 1093 (Wash, 1960).
77 Domino v. Mercurio, 234 NYS(2d) 1011 (1962).
78 McGee v. Board of Ed. of New York, 226 NYS(2d) 329 (1962).
79 Thurman v. Consolidated Sch. Dist. No. 128, Turpin, 94 FSupp 616 (Okla, 1950).

however, be held personally liable for injuries to students resulting from transportation accidents if arrangements for such transportation are made without the official approval of the board of education. A Wisconsin court ruled that a school district was not liable for the injuries sustained by a pupil of another school district who was invited by two coaches, without the knowledge or approval of the board of education, to travel to an extracurricular event on one of the school district's buses.[80] And in another case a teacher who permitted her automobile to be used by an athletic coach to transport players to a football game was held personally liable for the injuries sustained by a student when the automobile was involved in an accident.[81]

In cases involving injuries to spectators, the courts have ruled that a board of education can be held liable for negligence in relation to ministerial acts performed by the board of education or any of its agents,[82] but that it cannot be held liable for injuries inflicted by the unlawful or willful misconduct of its students in the absence of guilt for some act of commission or omission amounting to negligence.[83]

A California court held a school district liable for negligence because of its failure to anticipate the use of an abandoned broadjumping pit by a child who was injured while playing in the sand in the pit,[84] but another court ruled that a school district did not violate a safe place statute when an adult spectator was injured by falling from an elevated area in a school parking lot when he used the entrance to the boiler room instead of the public walk to the gymnasium door.[85]

---

[80] Huettner v. Eau Claire, 243 Wis 80, 9 NW(2d) 583 (1943).
[81] Gorton v. Doty, 69 P(2d) 136 (Idaho, 1937).
[82] Adams v. Schneider, 71 IndApp 249, 124 NE 718 (1919).
[83] Weldy v. Oakland High Sch. of Alameda County, 19 Cal App(2d) 429, 65 P(2d) 851 (1937); see also Hack v. Sacramento City Jr. College Dist. of Sacramento, 21 P(2d) 477 (Calif, 1933).
[84] Brown v. Oakland, 51 CalApp(2d) 150, 124 P(2d) 369 (1942).
[85] Hemmingway v. City of Janesville, 275 Wis 304, 81 NW(2d) 492 (1957).

Chapter 7

CONCLUDING SUMMARY

Extracurricular activities have been expanded to provide numerous educational experiences for youth. Today these activities are recognized by both legal and educational authorities as an important segment of the public school program.

In the course of conducting extracurricular activities, school districts and teachers become involved in legal problems, some of which come before the courts for adjudication. It is the purpose of this book to provide a body of knowledge relative to the legal status of extracurricular activities. From the cases discussed herein, the following conclusions are drawn:

1. The courts recognize competitive athletics as an integral part of the public school program.
2. School districts may expend public funds for the construction and maintenance of auditoriums, gymnasiums, and stadiums.
3. Boards of education may use their power of eminent domain to acquire land for the construction of athletic facilities.
4. School districts may enter into cooperative agreements with municipalities and other noneducational agencies for the financing of extracurricular activities.
5. The courts are in disagreement about the authority of school districts to purchase supplies, such as athletic clothing and band uniforms, for specific extracurricular activities, but in the most recent case the court upheld such an expenditure.
6. Although many school districts provide transportation for extracurricular groups, the legality of such an expenditure is questioned by some courts and attorneys general, and in the absence of a significant

number of cases in the area, no legal principle has been established.

7. School districts may use their facilities for athletic contests, dances, and other social activities.

8. Boards of education may charge a radio station fees for the privilege of broadcasting athletic events.

9. Extracurricular facilities may be leased to noneducational groups so long as the contract can be honored without interfering with the activities of the school.

10. Proceeds of extracurricular activities are public funds and must be accounted for in the same manner as all other school district funds.

11. School officials may prohibit secret society members from participating in extracurricular activities or from representing their schools in public contests, if membership in the secret society is proved to have detrimental effects on the good order and discipline of the school.

12. Students can be prohibited from participating in extracurricular activities for failing to sign a pledge stating that they are not members of a secret society.

13. The courts have upheld the authority of school boards to prohibit married students from participating in extracurricular activities, but there is some indication that this trend might be reversed.

14. Voluntary organizations, such as high school athletic associations, have no legal entity apart from their members, and must sue and be sued in the names of their members, unless a statute provides otherwise.

15. Before a school sues a voluntary association, of which it is a member, all remedies of appeal within the association must be exhausted.

16. School boards have the authority to permit schools under their direction to join high school athletic associations.

17. Upon joining a high school athletic association, a high school must abide by the rules and regulations of the association, or risk the penalty of suspension or expulsion.

18. The courts will not interfere with the operation of a high school athletic association so long as all internal activities are conducted according to the constitution and the by-laws of the association.

19. A high school athletic association can declare an athlete ineligible for interscholastic participation if the authority to do so is expressed in the constitution or by-laws of the organization.

20. A high school athletic association can regulate contracts made by member schools so long as provision for such regulations are present in the constitution or by-laws of the organization.

21. A high school athletic association has the authority to penalize members for the violation of rules and regulations so long as the penalties are provided for in the constitution or by-laws of the organization.

22. Although athletic coaches are subject to the same rules and regulations under their contracts as other teachers, their athletic duties are not always included under the teacher tenure laws.

23. Extra compensation, particularly honorariums, received by teachers for coaching duties are not always included in the teacher's salary total used for determining retirement benefits.

24. A board of education can assign teachers extracurricular duties for which they are qualified and certified so long as the activity is related to the school program and the general statutes and the teacher tenure laws are not violated.

25. If a teacher fails to perform extracurricular duties for which he is qualified and certified, he can be dismissed for willful and persistent negligence.

26. Although it has the authority to do so, a board of education does not have to give teachers extra compensation for extracurricular assignments.

27. In the absence of statutes or court decisions abrogating governmental immunity, school districts are not generally liable for the torts of their officers, agents, and employees.

28. In states where governmental immunity prevails, the courts have permitted recovery, in a few cases, for injuries which were sustained while the school district was engaged in what the courts defined as proprietary functions.

29. Although the consensus is not unanimous, the courts have generally ruled that a board of education does not act in a private or proprietary capacity by sponsoring profit-making enterprises of extracurricular activities.

30. Governmental immunity has been abrogated in the state of Washington except for accidents sustained in connection with athletic "apparatuses or appliances," but the courts have failed to arrive at a uniform definition of these terms, so no definite legal principle exists in this regard.

31. A teacher is not immune from presonal liability for acts of negligence while performing his duties, and his failure to supervise pupils adequately might constitute negligence on the part of the school district.

32. A teacher might be held personally liable for injuries sustained by a student injured in an accident while riding in the teacher's automobile on the way to or from an extracurricular event.

33. A school district, even under statutes abrogating governmental immunity, might not be held liable for injuries inflicted by the unlawful or willful misconduct of its pupils.

TABLE OF CASES

References are to sections.

165

Murphy v. Boston, 337 Mass 560, 150 NE(2d) 542 (1958), 5.2, 5.4

Nichols v. Calhoun, 204 Miss 291, 37 S(?d) 313 (1948), 2.2, 2.9

North Carolina Util Comm, State ex rel. v. McKinnon, 254 NC 1, 188 SE(2d) 134 (1961), 2.4, 2.8

Parrish v. Moss, 106 NYS(2d) 577 (1951), 5.3, 5.4

Pease v. Millcreek Tp Sch Dist, 195 A(2d) 104 (Pa, 1963), 5.3, 5.4

Petition of Auditors of Hatfield Tp Sch Dist, 161 PaSuper 388, 54 A(2d) 833 (1947), 2.8, 2.9

Ranier v. Board of Ed of Prestonsburg Independ Sch Dist of Floyd Co., 272 SW(2d) 577 (Ky, 1954), 2.2, 2.9

Reed v. Rhea County, 189 Tenn 247, 225 SW(2d) 49 (1949), 6.2, 6.4

Rhoades v. School Dist No. 9, Roosevelt County, 115 Mont 352, 142 P(2d) 890 (1943), 6.2, 6.4

Richards v. School Dist of Birmingham, 348 Mich 490, 83 NW(2d) 643 (1957), 6.2, 6.4

Robinson v. Illinois High School Assn, 45 IllApp(2d) 277, 195 NE(2d) 38 (1963), 4.3, 4.5

Royce Independ Sch Dist v. Reinhardt, 159 SW 1010 (Tex, 1913), 2.7, 2.9

Sawaya v. Tucson High Sch Dist No. 1 of Pima County, 78 Ariz 389, 281 P(2d) 105 (1955), 6.2, 6.4

Schmidt v. Blair, 203 Iowa 1016, 213 NW 593 (1927), 2.5, 2.9

School City of East Chicago v. Sigler, 219 Ind 9, 36 NE(2d) 760 (1941), 5.2

School Committee of Salem v. Gavin, 333 Mass 632, 132 NE(2d) 396 (1956), 5.2, 5.4

Shapiro, Matter of v. Board of Ed, 250 AppDiv 57, 293 NYS 603 (NY, 1937), 5.3

Sherwood v. Moxee Sch Dist No. 90, 363 P(2d) 138 (Wash, 1961), 6.3

Singleton v. Jackson Municipal Separate School Dist., 355 F(2d) 865 (1966), 3.1

Slater, State ex rel v. Smith, 142 S(2d) 767 (Fla, 1962), 5.2, 5.4

Snowden v. Kittitas County Sch Dist No. 401, 38 Wash(2d) 691, 231 P(2d) 621 (1951), 6.3, 6.4

Sorenson v. Christiansen, 72 Wash 16, 129 Pac 577 (1913), 2.2, 2.9

Southwestern Broadcasting Co. v. Oil Center Broadcasting Co., 210 SW(2d) 230 (Tex, 1947), 2.7, 2.9

Starkey v. Board of Ed of Davis County Sch Dist, 14 Utah(2d) 227, 381 P(2d) 718 (1963), 3.4, 3.5

State v. Judges of Court of Common Pleas, 19 OhioOp(2d) 52, 181 NE(2d) 262 (1962), 4.1, 4.3, 4.5

Wilson v. Graves County Bd. of Ed, 307 Ky 203, 210 SW(2d) 350 (1948), 2.3, 2.9

Woodsmall v. Mt. Diablo Unified Sch Dist, 10 CalRptr 447 (1961), 6.3

Woodson v. School Dist No. 28, Kingman Co., 127 Kan 651, 274 Pac 728 (1929), 2.2, 2.9

Wright v. Board of Ed of St. Louis, 295 Mo 466, 246 SW 43 (1922), 3.3, 3.5

Wright and Ditson v. Boston, 265 Mass 452, 164 NE 619 (1930), 2.4, 2.9

TABLE OF ATTORNEYS GENERAL OPINIONS

References are to sections.

171

LEGAL BIBLIOGRAPHY

American Digest System. By the Publisher's Editorial Staff, St. Paul, Minnesota: West Publishing Company.
Including:
Century Digest. Vol. 43, 1903. Digest of all reported cases from 1658 to 1896.
First Decennial Digest. Vol. 17, 1910. Digest of all reported cases from 1897 to 1906.
Second Decennial Digest. Vol. 20, 1922. Digest of all reported cases from 1906 to 1916.
Third Decennial Digest. Vol. 24, 1929. Digest of all reported cases from 1916 to 1926.
Fourth Decennial Digest. Vol. 27, 1938. Digest of all reported cases from 1926 to 1936.
Fifth Decennial Digest. Vol. 39, 1949. Digest of all reported cases from 1936 to 1946.
Sixth Decennial Digest. Vol. 26, 1958. Digest of all reported cases from 1946 to 1956.
General Digest. Published annually from 1956 to date, with monthly supplements.
American Jurisprudence. By the Publisher's Editorial Staff. Rochester, New York: The Lawyer's Co-operative Publishing Company. Vols. 6 and 47, 1943.
American Law Reports. By the Publisher's Editorial Staff. Rochester, New York: The Lawyer's Co-operative Publishing Company. Published annually since 1919.
Black's Law Dictionary (Fourth Edition). Edited by Henry C. Black. St. Paul: West Publishing Company, 1951.
Corpus Juris. Edited by William Mack and others. New York: The American Law Book Company, Vol. 56, 1932.
Corpus Juris Secundum. Edited by Francis J. Ludes and Harold J. Gilbert. New York: The American Law Book Company. Vols. 7, 78, and 79, 1952.
Miscellaneous reports: Delaware County Reports (Pennsylvania) and District and County Reports (Pennsylvania).
National Reporter System. St. Paul: West Publishing Company. 1879 and published to date with weekly advance sheets.
Including:
The Atlantic Reporter. Reports in full every decision of the courts of last resort of Connecticut, Delaware, Maine, Mary-

land, New Hampshire, New Jersey, Pennsylvania, Rhode Island, and Vermont from 1885 to date.

The California Reporter. Reports in full every decision of the California Supreme Court and lower courts of record in California from 1959 to date.

The Federal Reporter. Reports in full every decision of the United States District Courts and the United States Circuit Courts and other federal courts from 1880 to date.

The Federal Supplement. Reports in full every decision of the district courts of the United States since 1932, Court of Claims since 1932 to 1960, and United States Customs Court since 1949.

The New York Supplement. Reports in full every decision of the New York Court of Appeals and lower courts of record in New York from 1888 to date.

The North Eastern Reporter. Reports in full every decision of the courts of last resort of Illinois, Indiana, Massachusetts, New York, and Ohio from 1885 to date.

The North Western Reporter. Reports in full every decision of the courts of last resort in Iowa, Michigan, Minnesota, Nebraska, North Dakota, South Dakota, and Wisconsin from 1879 to date.

The Pacific Reporter. Reports in full every decision of the courts of last resort in Alaska, Arizona, California, Colorado, Hawaii, Idaho, Kansas, Montana, Nevada, New Mexico, Oklahoma, Oregon, Utah, Washington, and Wyoming from 1883 to date.

The South Eastern Reporter. Reports in full every decision of the courts of last resort in Georgia, North Carolina, South Carolina, Virginia, and West Virginia from 1887 to date.

The Southern Reporter. Reports in full every decision of the courts of last resort in Alabama, Florida, Louisiana, and Mississippi from 1887 to date.

The South Western Reporter. Reports in full every decision of the courts of last resort in Arkansas, Kentucky, Missouri, Tennessee, and Texas from 1886 to date.

Shepard's Reporter Citations. By the Publisher's Staff. Colorado Springs: Shepard's Citations, Inc.

SELECTED BIBLIOGRAPHY

Bolmeier, E. C. "Legality of Extra Assignments for Teachers" in Law and the School Principal. Cincinnati: The W. H. Anderson Co., 1961.

Bolmeier, E. C. "Legality and Propriety of School Board Regulations Designed to Govern High School Marriages," Proceedings of the Second School Law Conference, Appalachian State Teachers College. Boone, N. C.: Appalachian State Teachers College, 1963.

Burchinal, Lee G. "Do Restrictive Policies Curb Teen Marriages?" Overview, I (March, 1960), 72-73.

Cleetwood, Cleet C. "Legal Liability for Injuries Sustained in a Public School Program of Interscholastic Athletics," Unpublished Ed. D. Dissertation, Duke University, 1959.

Connecticut Interscholastic Athletic Conference, Constitution and By-Laws. Wethersfield, Connecticut: Connecticut Interscholastic Athletic Conference, 1964.

Doddridge, Delmar W. "Distinction Between Governmental and Proprietary Functions of Municipal Corporations," Michigan Law Review, XXIII (February, 1925), 325-38.

Edwards, Newton. The Court and the Public Schools. Chicago: The University of Chicago Press, 1956.

"Extra Pay for Extra Duties," National Education Association Research Bulletin, XLI (May, 1963), 50-51.

Flowers, Anne and Edward C. Bolmeier. Law and Pupil Control. Cincinnati, Ohio: The W. H. Anderson Co., 1964.

Fulbright, Evelyn R. and Edward C. Bolmeier. Courts and the Curriculum. Cincinnati: The W. H. Anderson Co., 1964.

Fuller, Edgar and A. James Casner. "Municipal Tort Liability in Operation," Harvard Law Review, LIV (January, 1941), 437-62.

Garber, Lee O. "At Last A Big Step Toward High School Athletics Clean-Up—With Court Approval," The Nation's Schools, LXX (December, 1962), 44.

Hamilton, R. R. "The Legal Status, Control and Use of Athletic and Other Extra-curricular Funds," The Bi-Weekly School Law Letter, II (September 18, 1952).

Hamilton, Robert R. and Paul R. Mort. The Law and Public Education. Brooklyn, N.Y.: The Foundation Press, Inc., 1959.

Kilzer, L. R., H. H. Stephenson, and H. O. Nordberg. Allied Activities in the Secondary School. New York: Harper and Bros., Publishers, 1956.

175

Landis, Judson T. "Attitudes and Policies Concerning Marriages Among High School Students," Marriage and Family Living, XVIII (May, 1956), 128-36.

Martin, David V. "Trends in Tort Liability of School Districts as Revealed by Court Decisions," Unpublished Ed. D. Dissertation, Duke University, 1962.

National Federation of State High School Athletic Associations, 1964-1965 Handbook. Chicago: National Federation of State High School Athletic Associations, 1965.

Sabers, Richard. "Constitutionality of the South Dakota Statute Making All Accredited High Schools Eligible for Membership in SDHSIAA," South Dakota Law Review, 10 (Spring 1965), pp. 102-119.

Seasongood, Murray. "Municipal Corporations: Objections to the Governmental or Proprietary Test," Virginia Law Review, XXII (June, 1936), 910-44.

Seitz, Reynolds C. "Legal Responsibility Under Tort Law of School Personnel and School Districts as Regards Negligent Conduct Toward Pupils," Hastings Law Journal, XV (May, 1964), 495-519.

Virginia High School League Handbook. Charlottesville, Va.: University of Virginia, 1963.

Why a CIAC? Wethersfield, Connecticut: Connecticut Interscholastic Athletic Conference, n.d.

Wyoming High School Activities Association Official Handbook. Cheyenne, Wyoming: Wyoming High School Athletic Association, n. d.

INDEX

References are to sections.

COURTS—Concluded
New York County, Supreme Court, 6.3
New York, Supreme Court, 6.3, 6.4
North Carolina, Supreme Court, 2.3, 2.5, 2.9, 3.3
Ohio, Supreme Court, 2.4, 4.2
Oklahoma, Supreme Court, 4.3
Oregon, Supreme Court, 3.2, 6.3
Pennsylvania
    Superior court, 2.8
    Supreme Court, 2.4, 5.3, 5.4, 6.1, 6.2, 6.4
Rhode Island, Supreme Court, 5.3, 5.4
Sacramento County, superior court (California), 5.3
St. Louis, circuit court, 3.3
Sedgwick, district court (Kansas), 3.3
South Carolina, Supreme Court, 2.7, 2.8, 2.9
South Dakota, Supreme Court, 6.3
Taylor County, district court (Texas), 3.3
Tennessee, Supreme Court, 3.2, 6.2
Texas
    Court of civil appeals, 2.7, 3.3, 3.4, 4.4
    Supreme Court, 4.4
Utah, Supreme Court, 2.5, 2.6, 3.4
Washington, Supreme Court, 3.3, 3.5, 6.3
West Virginia, Supreme Court of appeals, 4.3
Wexford County, circuit court (Michigan), 3.4
Wichita County, district court (Texas), 4.4
Winnebago County, circuit court (Illinois), 4.3
Wisconsin, Supreme Court, 6.3
Wyoming, Supreme Court, 2.6
EXTRACURRICULAR ACTIVITIES
Athletic club initiations, 6.3, 6.4
Athletic coaches, 5.2
Athletic control board, supervision of, 2.8
Athletic games, 2.5, 2.6, 2.7, 2.8, 2.9, 3.3, 3.4, 5.3, 6.2
Authority of school board to control, 3.2, 3.4
Bands, 1.1, 2.3, 2.9, 3.2, 3.4, 5.3
Baseball, 2.7, 6.3
Basketball, 2.4, 5.3, 6.2
Baton twirling, 6.2
Bowling, 5.3, 5.4
Boys' association, 3.4
Broadcast fees, 2.7, 4.4
Cheer leading, 3.4